Dedication

This book is dedicated with sincere admiration to all of the marketplace warriors who get up everyday and rise for the newest challenge. It is my hope and prayer that this book will remind you that you are not in this battle alone. There are many dedicated individuals who are standing by your side now, or will be in your future, and together you will take your territory for the kingdom. May the well of blessing be open upon you as you practice the principles you are about to read. Have fun my friends! I sure enjoyed the journey of writing this for all of us.

Endorsement

"Linda has done a tremendous job in presenting Marketplace Ministry in a refreshing, intelligent, inspiring manner in her new book, PayDay Principles. I highly recommend it to all who have an interest in Marketplace Ministry and who desire to have their business/career prosper. This book conveys the message in such a clear way that we intend to make this as part of our graduate curriculum in the future."
Dr. Gloria Kennedy, PhD.
Logos Graduate School Dean

Acknowledgements

As I think about every detail that has gone into the writing of this book I can't help but be humbled. I have spent countless hours and made more mistakes than I care to admit in my career, so why the lot fell to me to share my thoughts is still amazing. God truly is a God who extends grace and mercy beyond the limits of imagination.

This book has been a process for me and everyone involved. I could never truly express my gratitude in mere words to all of those who have impacted my life, and my career. Each of them has left an imprint on my heart and soul that will be felt in these pages and will forever be a part of who I am yet to become. It is always dangerous to list particular names because the fear exists that I will inadvertently miss a critical person in my journey to success. But, in this particular passage there are those that truly must be named as a vital thread in the principles presented in the following pages. These are the dear people that have walked alongside me during this process and heard my heartfelt cry to make a difference. They have supported me, prayed for me, and gently pushed me. Without them I would not have been able to finish this project.

A special thanks goes to **Rich Marshall** and **Valerie Zurn** and their team at ROI Leadership International. For years I have followed

Rich through his writing, devouring all of his material as soon as I could. He is one of the first people I sought out in my quest to find an answer for my marketplace endeavors. After reading his first book, **God at Work**, I reached out to him in an email and asked him to pray for my particular situation at the time. He not only prayed, and emailed a reply, but suggested other marketplace leaders in my area. Wow! What a great messenger for the kingdom. A simple thanks seems trite when a person has provided so much wisdom to a fellow marketplace minister. For the record Rich and Valerie….you guys are awesome. I hope everyone is able to see the impact you are continuing to make at ROI Leadership International. I encourage them to visit www.roili.com for more information.

My Family

First, I want to thank my husband Jim. He is my biggest fan, best friend and confidant for over 25 years. He has supported me on so many levels over the years and has proven to be a Godly husband and father. To have put up with someone as motivated as me has at times has been a challenge I'm sure, but he has been there cheering me on the entire way. Our lifetime together has been under the Lord's control every step of the way. It's been a great joy sharing these 25 years together. I look forward to at least 25 more. I love you.

Our two sons, Jason and Nathan continue to be a constant inspiration for me and keep my feet on the ground daily! You guys bless me beyond expression! I am honored to have the finest men in the world as part of my life. As you both continue in your selected paths and seek His destiny for your lives, it is my hope that these principles will give you strength and courage to make a difference for the Kingdom of God. I am thankful that God in all of His wisdom allowed me to be your Mom. You make me proud every single day! All of you have put up with a lot of long quiet hours on my behalf just to get this complete. I love all of you guys! Together, we will each advance forward and pursue our individual marketplace assignments as we plan for the future. www.helpingyouplan.com.

Jon Kocurek
Jon (our adopted son) you have honored us with accepting us into your life and allowing us the pleasure of mentoring you, loving you, and calling you son. We have watched in great anticipation as we have witnessed your growth into a true man of God. Thank you for allowing us to be a part of your life. Your tender heart and willingness to accept instruction as you chase after your God ordained purpose has been a great example to our boys and a joy to all of us. God has great things in store for you as you continue to lift your marketplace to His control. May God continue to bless all of your endeavors especially www.helpingyoutoday.com.

Patty House
I am truly blessed that God placed you as part of my family. You and I have been there together since the start and are more like twins than cousins. Thank you for all of the years of sharing our lives together. I do look forward to the journey ahead. I know it is filled with as much love as can possibly be conveyed!

Givvie and Leon Searcy
You are the greatest in-laws that anyone could ask for. You made me a part of the family from the first time we met. I love you (Mom and Dad). Thanks for your constant support.

Second, I have to say thanks to my dear friends who have kept me sane, supported me, and held me accountable. I love you all. Thank you:

Dianne Foster, M.D.
You have been one of my biggest encouragers and confidants! You are part of my covering and a friend that was sent direct from Heaven just for me. You traveled with me to countless locations to hear me deliver the same message. (You never once fell asleep. Thanks.) Those long drives in the wee hours of the morning will never be forgotten. You made me see the best, allowed me to grow and kept me grounded. I love you for it! Your steadfast friendship, faith and prayers, is a true testament to the marketplace in which you have

labored. You are a part of our family and our lives forever. It is my sincere wish that God will reward your faithfulness to His kingdom and grant you the desires of your heart. I look forward to sharing those moments with you and rejoicing! Thank you for offering your abilities in the marketplace as a woman, a physician, and a great friend. **dfoster@helpingyouplan.com**

Dawn Stallings, Founder of Golden Rule Broadcasting

It has been an honor serving with you and plowing the trenches of sales together. You allowed me to express my deepest thoughts, frustrations, and hopes and bonded with me in a way that I truly cannot express in words. We are like spirits and God has blessed me greatly with your friendship. Thanks for keeping me on track and believing in me. I love you. I also support you wholeheartedly in your effort to take your marketplace success and bless the lives of those who are often forgotten. God has blessed you with an outreach ministry that you love, Golden Rule Broadcasting, a compassion ministry dedicated to bringing comfort and strength to those neglected, particularly seniors. Our entire team is proud to support you at www.goldenrulebroadcasting.org. What a marketplace minister you have become!

Jackie Garner, Director of Women's Ministries, Lakewood Church

What an honor it was for you to agree to write the forward for this book. Your commitment to marketplace ministry and to me as a friend has been one of the highlights and blessings of my life. We have walked this journey of friendship together for over twenty years. You have been there to share my tears and rejoiced with me in every victory. Your friendship, council and mentorship are something that I will forever treasure. I look forward to great things in the future. Thank you from the bottom of my heart for your encouragement on this book. For all of the years that we have dreamed together, I look forward to many years ahead!

Dr. Gloria Kennedy, PhD., Academic Dean, Logos Graduate School, Florida

You have been a true mentor to me. You have allowed me to express my ideas and have encouraged me to follow them. You ignited the fire and the passion for this book and I thank you for making such a dynamic impact on my life. Your support of all of my activities has been the catalyst for me to believe in this project from the start. May God's blessings forever rest on all of your future plans and on all you are called to achieve.

Angie Lai-Zayas, M.D. and Joseph Sellin M.D.

A heart felt thank you, to you and your entire staff for all you have done for me over the years. Your dedication to my complex health issues is what has kept me alive and able to get this project complete. Both you and your team are the greatest blessing that I could have asked for in my continued care. Your compassion has often reminded me of the humanity of us all. To Barbara Bailey, R.N., Pauline Wilson, R.N., Karen McCollum, R.N., and Ladon Johnson, R.N., thanks for all of the years of keeping the wheels turning on my behalf.

Gina Rizzo, M.D.

Wow! You have plowed through countless chapters of this book with me and encouraged me the entire way. Thanks for your friendship and support. Your cheering me on helped me keep plugging away. I know that you have your own challenges since you have faced a battle with cancer with courage and strength, and I believe with you that you will fulfill all that God has in store for you. Since you are a survivor by nature I agree with you that you will have a long healthy life for you and your family. True to your commitment to those who may need encouragement, you graciously suggested that anyone looking for hope or a change that will propel them to the next level can email you at inwaiting@sbcglobal.com.

Margie Teel

You have become a dear friend and a sister. Thanks for always being there to hold me up and keep me going. I couldn't ask for anyone better to be a part of my life and to share my future. Your ability to read my mind and keep me organized and focused always astounds me. What would I do without you?

Clara Springer

Who knew that twenty-one years ago what started as a casual meeting in a La Maze class would grow into such a deep and lasting friendship. We have walked through triumphs and obstacles together knowing that our friendship was sealed the moment we bonded. You are a great testament to bringing healing to your workplace on a daily basis. Thanks for being there for me and for remaining such a faithful friend.

Linda Richardson

You have covered this project in prayer from the start. Thank you for speaking into my life and praying this through. I stand with you now in all that God has for your future. You are a true armor bearer for me. Although you were fighting your battle against brain cancer you still found the time to call and offer a prayer of support despite "the circumstances." Your excitement over the marketplace is a true blessing.

Pastors Blayne and Kim Schorr, Grace Community Church

You have been faithful friends for over twenty years and have been there when any of us needed you. Both of you have been a blessing to our entire family. In a world that is filled with conditional love and acceptance, it is such a joy to know that you love us no matter what! www.grace.tv

Pastors Greg & Gayla Holley, New Life Christian Fellowship

You are both Pastors that understand Marketplace Ministry and what a pivotal role that a marketplace leader has in kingdom economics. You took your place as the priests over many of my marketplace endeavors. Thank you for showing me the value of true covering over a business arena. I encourage people to visit your blogs at www.marketplacefaith.biz and www.gaylasmagazine.com .

Pastors Joe and Becky Keenan, Gulf Meadows Church

You guys truly have Pastor's hearts. You reached out to our

family and embraced us, prayed for us, covered us, and showed us the meaning of unconditional love during some of our darkest moments. Thanks for reminding us what a blessing the body of Christ can be to one another. You embraced the message of the marketplace and implemented it within your church and sphere of influence with passion. Thanks for being there to lend a hand when one was greatly needed for sharing and endorsing this message. www.gulfmeadowschurch.org

Roxanne Foster

What a great example to marketplace ministry you have become. Your commitment to the mission field after serving your marketplace has been a great testament to your faith. You have been faithful to cover us during this project and we look forward to many years of serving and supporting you in the future. We always look forward to the next time we get to spend some time with you. www.roxannedfoster.com

Libby Haynes, owner of Armoires and More, Dallas, Texas

You were the first to remind me that the message of the marketplace is truly needed. You faithfully sat in the teachings for over a year and put all of these principles to work within your own kingdom. You were the pivotal person who inspired me to continue on and finish. I am still standing with you in prayer that your business will continue to thrive and grow under your capable leadership! www.armoires-more.com

Dr. Lee Barker, D.C.

Thank you for understanding the nature of chronic pain and for the dramatic change you have made in my treatment process. Your persistence has been a Godsend. I encourage anyone who is dealing with a chronic illness and looking for hope to email you at lbarker@helpingyouplan.com . What a blessing you are!

Colleen Raijman, R.N.

You are a dear friend and I appreciate your support more than you know. You have seen me in some of the deepest trial periods and walked through each of them with me. Your courage in your moment of pain was strength to those around you. In spite of your own challenges, you persevered to be a beacon of hope within your sphere of influence. You too are now counted with the survivors of cancer. Way to go! You did it!

Jana Lackey

Despite your busy schedule in Africa you have been my friend for over thirty years. Thanks for remaining faithful and loving me through the many years we have walked this life together. When we were a lot younger we dreamed together. Now, let's continue to dream for the future. Your work in Africa is a testament to your faith. www.lovebotswana.org

Pastor Randy Free

You are the one who started it all! Thanks.

Forward

Do you know that what you do in the workplace has spiritual significance and impacts the Kingdom of God as much as what you do at church?

As a minister at Lakewood Church in Houston, Texas, and Director of Women's Ministry, I talk to thousands of men and women on a weekly basis. Many believe they go to work to make money so they can go to church and do what is "really important" in life. The majority of men and women in America work 40 hours a week, 47 weeks out of the year, yet understanding our spiritual position in the marketplace ***is the least explored topic***. Most of us who work outside the home actually spend more time at work than at home, and yet we take little time to understand what the marketplace is *really* all about. Over 50% of the 147 million people who work in America say they are Christians, yet they do not fully take the authority of God and live every hour of life advancing the Kingdom.

Every book I have ever read on the marketplace tells me how I should act at work, or what the Bible says about walking in integrity on the job, but in "PayDay Principles – Does what I do Really Matter," Linda Searcy has captured the heart of our Father and His principles that will revolutionize your thinking about the workplace.

I was on a plane heading for the next city with the Lakewood Church Tour when I began to read "PayDay Principles - Does what I do Really Matter," and I could not put it down! I read it for the entire two-and-half-hour plane ride and could hardly wait to get to the hotel to finish it. I was so fired up and excited about these principles and how to apply them to my life, I found myself writing in the margins, and planning how I would apply them to my work and home environment as well.

I am so delighted that my dear friend and colleague, Linda Searcy has written this liberating book. Linda has the ability to communicate the supernatural principles of God in a natural way that enables anyone to grab hold of them and apply them in real life situations. She shares her own life experiences with humor and candor that is so refreshing and relatable! I have known Linda for over 20 years and it has been my pleasure to work closely with her and to develop such a wonderful friendship. She is a woman of integrity with a God-given gift to communicate His principles.

No matter what your job is, no matter who you employer is, no matter what your title is, the principles in this book will elevate your thinking to the supernatural level that is our inheritance in Christ Jesus. The principles in this book will take you from working at the mercy of someone else, to walking in the authority that God has intended for you!

If you're ready to make the most of every hour of your life for the Kingdom of God, I invite you to turn the page and open your heart for a supernatural awakening as you discover "PayDay Principles – Does what I do Really Matter," as we prepare to impact the Marketplace for the Kingdom together.

May God bless each of you that embark on this journey!

Jackie Garner
Director of Women's Ministries
Lakewood Church
Houston, Texas

Table of Contents

Marketplace Introduction 1
Chapter One – What is the Marketplace 6
Chapter Two The Principle of the Marketplace – The Beginning...... 10
Chapter Three - The Principle of Creation 13
Chapter Four - The Principle of the Open Door 22
Chapter Five - The Principle of God's Economy 26
Chapter Six - The Principle of Foundation 47
Chapter Seven - The Principle of Marketplace Authority 62
Chapter Eight - The Principle of Accountability 73
Chapter Nine - The Principle of Covenant 86
Chapter Ten - The Principle of Favor 100
Chapter Eleven- The Principle of Proper Placement 104
Chapter Twelve- The Principle of Vision 113
Chapter Thirteen- The Principle of Positive Reinforcement 118
Chapter Fourteen- The Principle of Paying Attention 126
Chapter Fifteen - The Principle of A United Front 131
Chapter Sixteen - The Principle of Perception 137
Marketplace Conclusion 142

Marketplace Introduction

"For the Israelites will live many days without king or prince, without sacrifice or sacred stones, without ephod or idol. Afterward the Israelites will return and seek the Lord their God and David their king. They will come trembling to the Lord and to his blessings in the last days." (Hosea 3:4-5) (King James Version)

THE TIME FOR THE KINGS TO TAKE THEIR PLACE HAS COME!

First, let me thank you for picking up this book. No doubt there are probably a myriad of reasons that led you to crack the cover open. One of those reasons is probably because the mere thought of the possibility of divine intervention in your current professional life would be a dream come true. The hope that the possibility could turn into a reality is what has peaked your interest. You did not pick up this book by accident! If you keep reading, I promise that the words contained in the following pages will be like a refreshing wind over the parched reality that you call your job. These pages will encourage you to dream again. They will solidify your belief that God is supremely interested in what goes on in your professional life. In fact, without a doubt your success is one of the greatest representations of

His power to a hurting world. Thus, your success is VERY important to Him. It is, of course, the only way that some of the masses will ever experience the transformation that a true encounter with an almighty God can bring. Am I perfect? Without hesitation I can assure you I'm not. What makes this book different from any other? Well, I'm in the trenches with you. I'm not speaking from the lofty position of one who has "arrived". I get up every day and enter the hectic rat race just like you. I sit across the conference room tables and in the boardrooms trying to convince a client that our company really is the best choice. I enter the bidding wars right along with the rest of humanity. I have left those meetings with an air of confidence that left my competitors wondering. I have also left those meetings realizing that I should have depended more on God's divine plan rather than my own ideas.

Meetings such as these are what made me begin to question how much of my professional life I had truly turned over to His leading. I am keenly aware of what it takes to face the stark reality of the working world. What brought about the passion that you will experience in the next few pages? Well, the story will unfold as you continue to read.

I found myself facing circumstances within my professional life that demanded a change of thinking; you might even say a miracle. Throughout the course of my career I have relied heavily on my reputation alone to provide the contacts needed for positive business experiences. But the more I was exposed to life in the jungle called work, the more I realized how much I needed the hand of God to guide me into the right place at the right time. I also found myself facing the disturbing truth that Christians were often sorely lacking in their business integrity. It was at the hands of the so-called "Christians" that I experienced some of my greatest defeats and tests of mercy and grace. For me to continue the quest for a transformation within my professional sphere I really needed to find out for myself once and for all what God thought about the subject of work and the workplace. I needed answers. I needed a professional intervention from someone capable of divine miracles.

It was during one of these crisis periods in my career while driving down the road that I cried out to God and asked for His mercy and for His help. I found myself asking why and I let the cry of my heart finally be expressed. While sitting at a red light I found myself releasing the floodgates of all the frustration that had been building in me for a very long time. Before I realized it, I heard myself practically screaming in the car and begging God for an answer. It was out of those initial screams that the true passion for the marketplace was settled within me. Most of the lessons that I will share with you during our journey together are ones that I learned through some very trying times. I didn't have the luxury of a mentor. There was no one that took my hand and guided me or showed me the way. It was as if I understood in that moment in the car that this was a lesson that God wanted to teach me all by Himself. If you have ever been in that position in your walk with the Lord; you know this to be a place of great excitement and yet enormous requirements. For those of you who have been anointed to shine His light into the darkness of the world of commerce, you will find (if you haven't already) that God will hold you to a higher standard.

You must be willing to allow Him to clip off the rough edges and smooth out the tarnished places if you are to actually be released in the true authority that is waiting for you. If you are willing to humble yourself and learn from many of the rocky places that I have walked, perhaps I can spare you a bit of pain that always comes with growing. It is my prayer that the principles that I share in this book will only ignite in you the passion to fulfill your destiny.

Destiny for some is a scary thought. It is probably because it brings with it the realization that accountability will inevitably be required. For some, it seems impossible to attain the ultimate destiny of their true calling. Some of the struggle may have been fueled by the inability or lack of attention that the traditional church placed on a person's work endeavors. Most of us have never even had our work life addressed from the pulpit. If it was, it was usually in a passing comment. I had also fallen victim to the mentality of many of those within the traditional church walls who seemed to diminish my work life and concentrate solely on my "church" activities. This lack of attention spent on my effectiveness in my professional career left me confused. It was as if the success in the marketplace was seen as somehow less spiritual than the "churchly" duties to which I volunteered my time. Was I to apologize for my command of the business arena? I felt gifted toward the business world but often felt less "validated" by those in spiritual authority. Therefore, I found myself in a vicious circle of trying to "perform" within the church as well as within my career. In so doing, I opened myself up to frustration and complete burn out. I hope I can spare you from that awful trap. But again, out of the ashes of burn out a true passion for perfecting my personal mission and purpose was born. It was then that I truly felt the mantle and weight to bring the message of the marketplace to those who would listen.

When I finally embraced the fact that there really was something different about the anointing I experienced in the boardrooms of many companies, then the greatness that God had in store for me really began to take shape. What a great ride it has been! There have been times of magnificent victories and times of disappointing defeats. Through each experience I can truly say that the hand of God has been there all along.

Perhaps in our time together I can tell you what I did right and what I did wrong and help you in your own personal quest. Without a doubt there is one thing I know without the least bit of hesitation. God knows where you are right now!

He knows what your inner dreams and desires may entail. In fact, truth be known, He probably put them there. As we continue on together I will agree with you that the power of God will rejuvenate your energy and passion for the place to which you have been called. Your true blessing and destiny awaits you as you continue on your journey.

It is my prayer that this book will validate you and encourage you to embrace your profession, your career, and the talents that lie within your grasp. Stop apologizing for your gifting! Don't feel embarrassed anymore about the success you experience in your personal career. The marketplace is the true calling and destiny for those of us who are gifted in this arena. The greatest miracles and witty strategies and inventions are still in store. How do I know that God really cares about where you are? Well, my friend, I'm there with you right now. In fact, at this very moment I am sitting at a local coffee shop waiting on a business appointment to arrive.

One of the ironic things is that sitting next to me right now are two gentlemen, dressed in business attire, taking a bit of a break from their "business" discussion to chat about their faith. What a small world it really is. Based on their conversation, they too seem to be seeking a divine hand to guide their daily activities. They are in need of a miracle in one of the deals that they are facing at work. So, the story is not unique. It is felt by all of those who wake up every morning to face another day at the office. Perhaps it can serve as a simple reminder that there are many of us in the ranks of the working world. Only we can choose how dedicated we will be to the pursuit of God's ultimate place for us. I salute you on your journey. Now, join me on the ride of our lives!

Chapter One – What is the Marketplace

The term marketplace is one of the hottest catch phrases of modern day. In fact, it is thrown around about as often now as someone "biggie sizing" the order at his or her favorite fast food chain. The complete sanctity of its office can easily be lost in the translation. However, there are distinct formulas for success both logically and spiritually. According to Webster the term marketplace means, "***a place where goods are traded; a distinct domain***." **(Webster's Pocket Dictionary, Pg. 245)**

As we look at the second part of the definition we begin to get a small glimpse into the whole picture. There are definite areas of business in which each of us are anointed or gifted. If we stay focused on that gifting, we can soar to unimaginable heights. Ephesians 3:20 is an interesting scripture. It says,

> **"Now, unto him that is able to do exceeding, abundantly, above all that we ask or think, according to the power that worketh in us." (King James Version)**

Most of us have heard this message preached with the emphasis placed on Him who is able. While I in no way seek to diminish the power of God in our lives, I find it interesting that the true message of the scripture has been watered down for a more palatable doctrine. The true action and emphasis in this scripture is actually on the power that **we** allow to work **inside** us. That, my friend, is what makes the difference for us. It is what truly defines us and gives us the distinct domain to which Webster is referring. The dominion that we have within our sphere of influence is directly affected and controlled by the things that we allow to "work" within our spiritual and professional lives.

According to a correct biblical perspective those two areas of our life were never meant to be separated. God's original intent has always been for us to have dominion within our marketplace endeavors equal to that within our own spiritual lives. Since the beginning man was made to walk in dominion. I have seen numerous books, and been to many seminars touting the "marketplace" as of late. However, the real message of the marketplace must first begin in a transforming process within our heart and life. The marketplace is waiting for the change to begin in you. The economy and practices of "doing business" are basically the same all over the world. What makes the difference are those of us who chose to operate within a different set of governing "parameters". This is true transformation. This is our ultimate purpose! God has put us in our own personal marketplace of dominion so that we may bring about transformation within that arena while adding provision and validity to God's kingdom.

Many of you have been struggling trying to "find" your place. Perhaps you have felt insignificant because you didn't feel like your business expertise was in any way an asset to the body of Christ. However, the power of the marketplace authority and gifting that is within you should free you to rise to your full potential as an ambassador for Christ within the sphere of influence in which you have been placed. All of us have a place that is divinely ordained as our "territory" and circle of authority. 2 Corinthians 10:13 says,

"We, however, will not boast beyond measure, but

> **within the limits of the sphere which God appointed us…"**

It is critical that we fully understand our calling and our potential within our place of assignment. It is God that has called us to follow in the footsteps of Christ. Since we know that Christ walks in all wisdom, power and authority, then we have free access to that supernatural power through our relationship with Him.

This power will enable us to stand fast in our faith and shine as a true testament and example to the overcoming power of a life that is totally dedicated to pleasing God. We must be willing to bring the nature and characteristics of God to every place we influence within our workplace and surrounding areas. In some cases the example we portray of Christianity will be the only point of reference that some will ever see. Simply stated, the world must recognize a difference in how you conduct your daily affairs of business. Your business ethics and code of conduct will directly affect the domain to which you have been assigned. It will also impact the extent of your dominion within that space.

The contents of this book are meant to form a commentary on the events and habits that must occur **within** you before the marketplace that you find yourself in is truly changed. Are you looking to expand your territory? Are you wondering why things just aren't working out for you? Do you find yourself struggling to make a difference? If some or all of these statements reflect any of your current thoughts, then this book is for you. It is my utmost prayer that as you prayerfully consider your business life you will gain the insight that you so desperately need. It is my belief that from this moment forward the change is already beginning. Now, let's explore together the elements needed for God's hand of blessing upon our business affairs.

<u>FIRST LESSON</u>: I MUST FIND MY PLACE IN THE MARKETPLACE.

<u>Questions to consider:</u>

1.) Do you know where you belong in the kingdom?
2.) Has true transformation begun in your heart?
3.) Can you identify your personal passion as it relates to your marketplace?
4.) Have you asked for God's hand of blessing to rest upon your business endeavors? If not, why not now?

Chapter Two - The Principle of the Marketplace – The Beginning

Have you ever wondered who performed the first "work" day in the world? Ok, since we are just getting started I'll help you. It was God. How about that? God is the one who started this entire work process. Genesis 2:2 says,

> **"And on the seventh day God ended his work which he had made; and he rested on the seventh day from all his work which he had made." (King James Version)**

So now that we know who is responsible, let's get down to understanding the work process and how God fits in. Did you know that God wants you to be able to look at your work life and be proud of what you have accomplished? How many of you can look at yourself and be honest and say that your current work environment is pleasing to God? If you answered yes, way to go! If you didn't answer yet, don't be discouraged. We are going to work through some thoughts together and improve your current conditions.

Let's look at how God approached His professional life. Did you know that He took time to examine what kind of a job He did? If all of us did this more often we could make necessary adjustments before they became too painful. The 31st verse of chapter one of Genesis is our first clue into the priority God places on a job well done. It explains the examination process that God did and His subsequent pleasure at a job well done. How many times have you thrown something together at the last minute and then prayed a hasty prayer for God's blessing? If we are truly going to expect God to "anoint" and "bless" us in our professional lives then we may need to fine-tune some of our work habits. So, a key lesson in our journey for God's favor is found in doing a job that will be a statement of our commitment and dedication to excellence.

To some this little reminder may seem trivial or unnecessary. However, how many times have you stayed a bit longer than you should have at lunch thinking it really didn't matter? How many times have you turned a report in late saying you just didn't have enough time when you knew how much time you really wasted? This is not meant as a condemnation. It only serves to jog you into a peak performance mentality. If you think that little things don't really matter, tell that to someone who only needs one gallon of gas to make it to the next filling station. One gallon of gas is worth a million bucks when you have to walk four or five miles to remedy your situation. Tell that to someone who only needs one blood transfusion to survive. Little things do make a difference. Many times they make the difference or the determination as to whether we win or lose.

Sometimes it's the minor adjustments that can make or break a sale. Remember that the next time you are talking on a cell phone and hear yourself repeating the all too familiar line, "can you hear me now". The point is that your job is just one piece of a master puzzle. Without your particular piece, the puzzle cannot be finished. Think about that the next time you perform some seemingly meaningless task. Did you ever think that if that fax or package did not get there on time what would happen? What about if that one phone message didn't reach your boss in time? What about the importance of making sure that everyone else has everything they need to do their job? You are important no matter what it is you do. **You are the piece of someone's puzzle.**

The second lesson in the study of the beginning stages of work is God's creative process. I can't tell you enough how comforting this is for me. As a sales professional, I am often asked to deliver what might as well be the miracle of the Red Sea. In a declining economy I am still expected to produce more than I did last year, at a higher profit margin, even though competition is increasing and cost of goods is expanding almost exponentially. Go figure. So, in order to say that I am truly blessed in my endeavors I need a creative miracle from God on a daily basis!

I need Him to create a budget where there is none. I need Him to create a project where there is none. I need Him to help me figure out ways to squeeze out more and more profit. I need Him to bring my proposal to the forefront over any of my competitors. I need Him to expose any deception that my competitors may be trying in order to win the business. I need Him to open doors into new markets and territories and give our company the skill and favor to move in that direction. Well, you get the picture. I (and you) need the creative power of God to be evident within our marketplace.

SECOND LESSON: I MUST DO A JOB THAT IS EXCELLENT AND IN WHICH I CAN BE PROUD.

Questions to consider:

1.) Have you gained a greater appreciation for your workplace as a Result of God's example?
2.) Are you currently proud of your work performance?
3.) Can you identify any actions that are necessary to refine your work skills?
4.) Do you see where you "fit" on your current team?

Chapter Three - The Principle of Creation

Creation can be thought of in two ways. There is a supernatural creation and a natural creation. Both of them will require divine intervention for them to make a lasting impression within our marketplace. Let's examine them both together. Hang tight with me here just for a moment and it will become clear.

Supernatural Creation – This is truly a miracle. This is when something is formed or created out of nothing. The word nothing represents zero. How many times have you heard someone whisper to you, "Now there goes a big fat zero"? It doesn't take an interpreter to figure out what is meant by that statement. A zero is something that is seen as having no potential. From a simplistic mathematical perspective when zero is added to anything the net effect has not changed. For example, 2 + 0 = 2. There was no change. Everything is the same. That may be how some of you are feeling at this very moment. You may feel like a big zero sitting out there with no potential for greatness. Even worse, you may think that others think of you in that light as well.

However, let's turn the equation around. If you add something to zero what do you get? Let's take the same equation from above with one "minor" adjustment. 0 by itself is nothing right? How about if we do this….0 + 2 = 2. When we added 2 to 0, we got the desired result. We had an increase. That's right….we got a change. Perhaps part of the problem within your thought process at the moment is that you have been trying to add yourself (the zero) to something, and now you don't feel like anything is happening. The sad truth is that probably nothing is. But, if you will take just a moment and think about what could change if you added God to your personal equation your world will never be the same. It will be a different story. When God is allowed access to the equation of our lives it is certain that an increase will occur. God is all about INCREASE.! Deuteronomy 16:15 reminds us,

> **"…because the Lord thy God shall bless thee in all thine increase, and in all the works of thine hands, therefore thou shalt surely rejoice."**

When you add God to your business and professional career, you have now added the Creator, the Giver of life, to the zero that you may feel like at this moment. Something plus zero is still an increase, right? Get the picture? Stop trying so hard to put yourself in the equation. The important thing is that God is allowed to enter. That is when the net effect will begin to be noticeable. Start adding God to your job and bingo….the creativity begins. Remember, it was God who created something from nothing. (The earth was without form when He started. It was a big void….a big fat nothing.) You can read the entire story in Genesis chapter one.

WHEN I ADD GOD TO MY BUSINESS EQUATION THEN I CAN BE ASSURED THAT INCREASE IS JUST AROUND THE CORNER!

Natural Creation: This one is a bit easier to understand. Natural creation occurs when things that already exist are added to each other to form something new. You may need a new idea, slogan, project methodology, etc. Sometimes the answer may lie in combining a myriad of successful techniques that you are already using to produce a new workflow.

Have you ever found yourself sitting in a quiet moment, perhaps at work, in your car, at home, wherever and wishing somehow that God could reach into your brain and just tell you what to do? Have you ever wished that he would just magically appear in front of you and lay out a plan for you that made sense? Come on….I can't be the only one who has ever wished for this! Have you tried in vain to master the "gimmicks" of the latest fad only to realize that they just don't quite fit your particular segment of the market? Maybe, they don't fit into your own personal value system. Or perhaps, the implementation costs of some of these "guaranteed" programs, is just beyond your reach. Here we are again at a place in your career and/or life where you need a miracle to occur if you are to survive.

Here's the good news, I have personally witnessed the miracle hand of God in many situations throughout my career. An even better bonus is that He doesn't require an exorbitant fee in order to get His advice, opinion or council. His only requirement is that you allow Him complete control of your professional activities and behavior.

Now, let me be the first to point out that this isn't free. It is presenting our lives to Him daily as an investment in our future. Consider it the first "day trading" activities in history. In God's economy there is no greater guarantee of return that is greater than that! He will require sacrifice. He will require obedience. He will require ethical behavior. But, the pay off is well worth any investment you make. Are you in a place now where you find yourself lagging behind your competition? Do they seem one step ahead of you in quality, price and delivery? Have you been crying out to God for a solution to the bottom line dilemma that your Profit and Loss statement is showing? Is cash flow stretching you to the breaking point? Have you found yourself beginning to doubt that your faith really can make the difference for you and your business? Do you need a miracle idea from Heaven to survive?

Here's the good news, God promises to give you all the knowledge that you need. Are you ready to start making the change right now? Let's start simple. How about right now you say a little prayer with me as we get started? It doesn't have to be this exact one but maybe this one will help get you started.

> **"God, first I want to ask you to forgive me for not coming to you sooner and asking for your help in my business and professional career. Right now, for anything I may have done that was not totally pleasing to you, I ask for forgiveness. From this moment forward I am giving my professional career over to you. I ask you to help me with the knowledge and wisdom necessary to succeed while still bringing glory to your name. Help me to be a better employee, a better boss, a better owner, and a better witness of your power within my marketplace. I ask for Divine guidance, inventions, and strategies that will help increase all that you have placed in my hand.**
> **In Jesus name. Amen.**

If you just prayed that prayer then congratulations! You are well on your way to see the increase that you so desire. **Proverbs 8:12 says, "I wisdom dwell with prudence, and find out knowledge of witty inventions." When you ask God to get involved in your life and give you wisdom, He promises to give you knowledge of "witty inventions".**

So from now on keep a journal of every idea that may pop into your head. Remember, it only takes one idea to get you back on top of the game. You are only one invention, thought or idea away from gaining additional increase. Ask for the ***miracle of natural increase*** over your business right now. Ask God to nudge you with His ideas on how to improve your situation. If you truly don't know what to do next then just be honest with God and tell Him. After all, just a few moments ago you invited Him into your business career. You asked Him to help you to be a better witness of His power in the marketplace. When you do that, then His name is at stake as well as yours! James 1:5 in the Amplified says,

> **"If any of you is deficient in wisdom, let him ask of the giving God (who gives) to every one liberally and ungrudgingly, without reproaching or faultfinding, and it will be given him."**

In other words, if you can't figure it out, ask Him to help. He wants to give you the ideas and wisdom that you need. In many cases the answer may already be staring you in the face. You probably already have the team of individuals or products that you could rearrange that would produce an unbelievable result. Start keeping your eyes open and your mind ready to receive His instruction. Remember how many different successes Jacob had with the same flock of sheep? We will study that in depth a bit later. Just hang on, help is on the way!

Speaking of what you may already have, let's talk about the team approach. One of the easiest biblical examples of natural creation is the formation of the "team" of disciples. Jesus took a dozen business professionals of His day and created one of the most memorable teams of all time. He managed a group of men that literally changed the world! How would you like that on your managerial resume? In fact, most of us would have probably chosen a few more "seasoned" and "professional" guys to get the job done. But, through the natural creation miracle Jesus proved that you really could use a bunch of business people to get the job done. ☺ See, we really are able to impact the world in more than monetary ways! Are you starting to feel more important yet?

The faster you realize that God has everything under control, the less stressed out you will feel. Let's face it, most people operate with the same basic set of social graces, rules, etc. What makes you any different than anyone else? It's simple. The difference happens when His creative process is allowed to take root in your thinking. He thinks differently than we do. He knows that His words bring to life the creative process. **His words have the power of creation.**

"He spoke, and it was created." (Psalm 33:9)

To further emphasize this point Hebrews 11:3 in the Amplified Bible reminds us that the very word of God is what equips us and frames our destiny. It says,

> **"By faith we understand that the worlds were framed, fashioned, put in order and equipped for their intended purpose by the WORD of God, so that what we see was not made out of things which are visible."**

In a nutshell, it means that our words are what help form the things in our lives, which are considered tangible. Although you cannot feel or touch a word, it does have the power to produce something for you in your physical world of existence. What would happen if everything you said actually came true? For most of us that might be a scary thought! When I realized the true power of the spoken word I became much more careful about all the things I let fly out of my mouth. I keep my mouth shut a lot more and stop many comments before they get past my big mouth. Some of you would do much better if you practiced this habit. Our spoken word reinforces an idea within our subconscious mind. In fact, Jesus thought so much of the words that we allow to flow from our lips that He said they would judge us. He said:

> **"But I say to you that for every idle word men may speak, they will give account of it in the day of judgment.**
> **For by your words you will be justified, and by your words you will be condemned." (Mathew 12:36)**

What are you speaking over your business endeavors at the moment? Are you speaking words of life? Are you speaking things that you want to happen? One of the most enlightening exercises in your journey is to visualize in your mind all the things that you have spoken regarding your professional career. As you think of the images, are they negative or positive? Are they the thoughts of a winner? If you knew that everything you professed over your career would come true, would you change some of the things you say? Think about it. I encourage you to read the first chapter of John. It is an awe-inspiring chapter of the power of God and His Word. The chapter begins by establishing that the Word (Jesus) was with God from the beginning. Verse three of that chapter says, **"Through him all things were made; without him nothing was made that has been made."** If you continue reading the fourteenth verse states, **"The Word became flesh and made His dwelling among us."**

If you knew right now that the words that you had spoken over your business would take physical form around you would you start running or would you be at peace? Notice that the scripture reminds us that nothing in our own physical realm was made without the assistance of the word. I fully understand that these passages of scripture are reminding us that Jesus is the Word. However, it is also a great reminder for all of us to adequately understand the power that the spoken word has in the fulfillment of our destiny. For some of you the greatest enemy in your life at the moment is your own tongue. You have been cursing your own deals and speaking death to some of the contracts that should have rightfully been yours. For the moment, as you are learning about authority, ask for God's help to speak words of life over everything pertaining to your family, business and personal affairs.

So how do we get control of our tongue? My personal motto…when in doubt; just don't speak. Jesus knew the power of the spoken word. He understood its power to bring life and its ability to create consequences. He guarded what He spoke. Remember the story of the fig tree? All it took was one word from Him for the tree to stop producing fruit. Now that is what I call power! What have you spoken to that has stopped producing fruit? Perhaps you didn't even realize that you were actually cursing your own harvest.

The words we speak are critical to our success. One of our most vulnerable times are those moments when we are frustrated, tired, are at an emotional low. This is when we can really make some mistakes in our proclamations over our business endeavors. If you are in the place at this moment when you feel overwhelmed by the sheer reality of your circumstances, then stop and take a moment to quiet your mind and your mouth. This could be one of the greatest lessons you will ever learn.

When Satan confronted Jesus in the wilderness I think we could all agree that Jesus was at a place physically, spiritually, and emotionally where He was at the last end of His rope. He was spent. He had been in that desert for 40 days with that varmint Satan hanging around and harassing Him at every turn. To make matters even worse Jesus knew that in one split second He could get an immediate assist from 10,000 angels if He so desired. He also knew that He could smash His tormentor to a pulp if He truly wanted. (Believe me, this would have probably been my first thought) However, He was smart enough to speak only the Word of God. That is the only answer He gave to the accuser. Just the Word. Only the Word. No commentaries. No opinions. No summaries. Just the Word of God. Wow, what a lesson. In our moments of deepest trial, temptation and despair we should follow the example of Jesus! That is when we can potentially make or break what God is trying to work in our lives. You will never go wrong if you speak the Word!

Take a moment right now and think about the conversations and words that you have been speaking just over the past 30 days. Have they been words of life? Would they invoke a blessing to come your way? If not, then stop speaking! Let's take a moment right now together to once again begin fresh in our marketplace. Pray right now and ask God to break the bondage and damage that any of your negative words may have caused. Ask Him to give you the words to speak over your current situation and to bless your endeavors as you seek to honor Him. Now, sit back and watch the power that His word can bring.

<u>THIRD LESSON</u>: I MUST ALLOW THE CREATIVE WORK OF GOD TO BE PRESENT IN MY PROFESSIONAL LIFE.

<u>Questions to consider:</u>

1.) Can you see the potential of allowing God to have control of your business life?
2.) Can you already identify some things in your daily activities that need to change in order to give Him full power?
3.) Can you identify areas within your life where you need a miracle?
4.) Can you identify any negative words that may have affected the outcome of some of your transactions?
5.) If so, take time right now to write down these items and then speak the direct positive to those particular items.

Chapter Four - The Principle of the Open Door

As we look at our life in the business realm one of the greatest assets is having an ability to open the door into a new territory. These open doors may represent new ideas, new accounts, new product development, etc. For any business to survive it is critical that the boundaries and marketplace territories are always expanding. In many cases this expansion can only occur with a divine intervention of some sort. How many times have you found yourself with your back against a wall facing what seemed like an insurmountable situation in front of you? You feel the struggle for advancement on your shoulders encroaching on every fiber of faith within your being. When you find yourself in these situations it is important to remember ***The Principle of the Open Door.***

Do you realize that God wants to empower you with the authority needed for every situation? He gets no glory if you don't realize your potential. He has equipped you with the tools you need to walk in that authority. Let's look at how God sees the situation. He says,

> **"In that day I will summon my servant, Eliakim son of Hilkiah. I will clothe him with your robe and fasten your sash around him and hand your**

> **authority over to him.**
> **He will be a father to those who live in Jerusalem and to the house of Judah. I will place on his shoulder the key to the house of David: what he opens no one can shut, and what he shuts no one can open. I will drive him like a peg into a firm place…" Isaiah 22:20-23**

As you approach the daily activities within your career wouldn't it be nice to know that you had the ability to walk into supernatural provision? According to the scripture above we learn that when God places the mantle of authority upon our shoulders ***The Principle of the Open Door*** begins to unfold. When we turn the controls of our life over to Him, we can rest in the fact the God begins to go ahead of us in every situation. Once He props the door open for us we know that it cannot be shut without His approval. What a great comfort. This should encourage you as well. Have you been beating your head against the wall or found yourself banging on the door of success? When God is involved a little nudge may be all you need to get the door open. Stop right now and think about your situation. Do you feel as if you have been jamming the wrong key in the door lock only to find that the door won't open? First, are you sure you are at the right door? Take this moment right now and ask God to manifest ***The Principle of the Open Door*** on your behalf. Perhaps He's just waiting on you to stop pounding on the door and let Him have control. (just a thought)

When Joshua first saw the land of promise he recognized that there were "giants" in the land. However, when he gave his report to the weekly strategy meeting he wasn't deterred in the least. He acknowledged that there were obstacles ahead, but reminded those in leadership that the Lord had already declared the victory for them. He also remembered that God had already promised him that every place his foot touched would be his. Joshua 1:3 in the Amplified says,

> **"Every place upon which the sole of your foot shall tread, that I have given to you…"**

I have often used this scripture to comfort me as I faced obstacles that seemed almost too large to handle. As I have entered new cities or territories for my company I remind the Lord that my marketplace belongs to Him. As long as I dedicate my efforts to Him I leave the results in His capable hands. After all, as I, and my company advance and increase, so does His kingdom. He wants me (and you) to succeed. It is His desire that ***The Principle of the Open Door*** operates within our sphere of influence.

You must begin to realize the power that rests within you as you dedicate everything to Him. As you continually put His word in your mind and trust Him for the outcome you will be able to experience the promise of Joshua 1:8 just as Joshua did. The Amplified says it this way:

> **"This book of the law shall not depart out of your mouth, but you shall meditate on it day, and night, that you may observe and do according to all that is written in it; for then you shall make your way prosperous, and then you shall deal wisely and have good success."**

If you are an employee of a company begin to pray for open doors. This will mean you have favor to excel above all of your competitors. If you are the business owner, pray that you and your employees walk in this principle. If you already have an employee that seems to walk through places that no one else can get through, then acknowledge that this employee is operating under the anointing of ***The Principle of the Open Door*** and guard that employee with everything you have. This employee is someone who has already tapped into the promises of God for their future and yours.

<u>FOURTH LESSON</u>: I MUST SEEK TO FOLLOW IN THE PATH OF THE PRINCIPLE OF THE OPEN DOOR.

<u>Questions to consider:</u>

1.) Do you operate with the Principle of the Open Door in mind or do you force your way into certain situations?
2.) Do you allow God to Open the doors for you that He wants you to walk through instead of opening them for yourself?
3.) When was the last time you asked God to open the doors He wanted you to walk through and shut all others?
4.) Do you have an employee or teammate that is gifted in this particular area? If so, USE THEM!

Chapter Five - The Principle of God's Economy

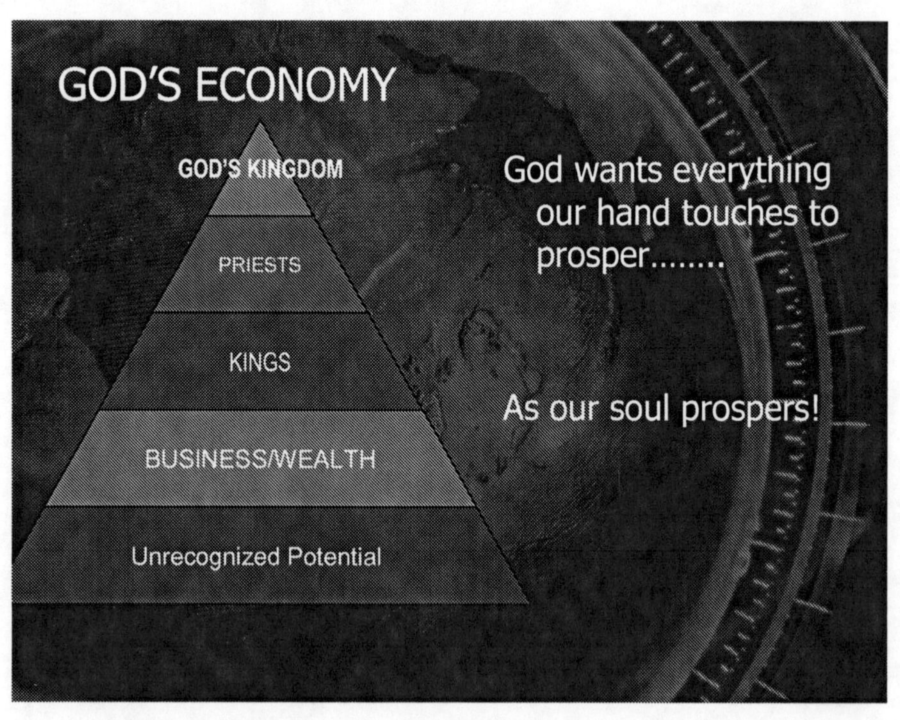

> **"Beloved, I pray that you may prosper in all things and be in health, just as your soul prospers." (3 John 2)**

The economy of God is really quite simple to understand. If you can grasp the principles that follow, then you will not have to worry about lack or what the current trending in the market may indicate. You can know beforehand when and how to make a change that will propel your business to the next level.

First, let me remind you that it is God's ultimate desire to prosper you and bless you so that His kingdom may advance. He longs for you to find your full potential and walk into the destiny that He has designed for you. With that in mind, there are five basic elements to the marketplace of God. Let's consider them together.

They are:

1.) Unrecognized Potential
2.) Business and Wealth
3.) Kings
4.) Priests
5.) God's Kingdom

All of these elements make up the marketplace economy of God. Each of them has a special and unique feature and/or gifting that will help us survive in the world of business. Let's start with the basics and then move forward.

Through the study of scripture it is evident that God places a lot of emphasis on authority, and organizational structure. We could spend an entire book on that subject alone. However, for the purposes of understanding His economy as it pertains to our business life, let's just keep it simple. The figure at the beginning of this chapter displays the simple order of our professional lives. All of us begin on the bottom rung of this diagram. It is the area of unrecognized potential. Please note, that God wants us to move past this area into a more fulfilled life. But, let's start with that area and then move forward.

Unrecognized Potential

Sadly, many people stay in this arena their whole lives, professionally, spiritually and personally. They never seem to "measure up" to the demands of their busy schedule or the constant comparisons that they make between themselves and their peers. Very few people actually step out of this stage of life to pursue their talents and skills while at the same time refining the gifts that have been placed within them. The Word of God is very specific about when God first places His hand upon your life. The Amplified Bible shows us in Jeremiah 1:5 by reminding us the words of God to Jeremiah. They are:

> **"Before I formed you in the womb I knew and approved of you (as my chosen instrument), and before you were born I separated and set you apart, consecrating you, and I appointed you a prophet to the nations."**

For just a moment get your mind quiet. Empty your mind of every thought. Now, if I were sitting with you right now and were to ask you what you thought your gifts and talents were, could you honestly tell me? If I asked you how you felt you measured up to the potential within you, could you give me an answer? What if I asked you an even more vulnerable question?

Do you think that God approves of you right now? You may be thinking that this is getting into a little too deep. But, you must settle this issue once and for all if you are to realize your true destiny. Let's look at the questions together.

1.) **What are your gifts and talents?** - These are easily defined as those things at which you excel. They are the things that excite you the most and that produce the most passion and happiness for you. Perhaps it is music, art, literature, organizational skills, sales, hospitality, medicine, or working with your hands. Whatever it is, it will be the key to unlock the door of hidden potential within. Start doing a personal inventory to see what things make you the happiest and begin to write those down in your journal as well. You are better at some things than others. What are they?

2.) **<u>Do you feel you measure up?</u>** - Again, this question is only meant to gently nudge you to ensure that you deal with any issues that may be holding you back. Perhaps you have made it through life accidentally thus far. In other words, you haven't applied yourself fully. Only you know the answer. If you were to get an invisible measuring tape and mark where you think you are as to where you think you should be, what would the measurement indicate? Is it time to make some small adjustments to begin to strengthen those gifts that are inside? Hint, you are doing a positive thing right now by reading this book! What other activities would you say you do that will directly affect your life in a positive way?

3.) **<u>Do you think God approves of you right now?</u>** - For some of you this may be the hardest question of all. Most of us automatically think that we can never truly please God. You may already be dealing with feelings of inadequacy in other areas of your life. But, let me take you back to God's words to Jeremiah. A loving Father saw Jeremiah, while he was still in his mother's womb. God was there at the very moment that Jeremiah's life began. In fact, it was at that very moment that God approved of Him and selected Him as His chosen instrument. The hardest concept for many of us to grasp is that God can love us despite our imperfections and mistakes. He is more than willing to take a willing vessel and use it for His kingdom purposes. You may be feeling like that there is no redemption for the past that haunts you. But, God see past your defeat and proclaims victory to your future. Settle one thing once and for all in your mind. God loves you.

When you give everything over to His control he sees you, and He works on your behalf because He approves of you. Just think, God cared enough to take notice of you as you were conceived. It was at that first moment of your life that He placed talents and gifts within you that would shape the destiny that He felt belonged to you and only you. It should be a revelation to you as to how much God wants to be involved in your life. God is proud of you. He loves you, and He wants to work strong in your behalf in every part of your life. To finish this thought process let's look at one of my favorite scriptures. Jeremiah 29:11 says,

> **"For I know the thoughts that I think toward you says the Lord. Thoughts of good and not of evil, to give you a future and a hope."**

God is all about making sure that your future is secure. So, settle in your own mind for all eternity that God approves of you and truly wants to bless you. It is through you that his kingdom will be established upon this earth.

So, here we are at the end of this particular rung of the ladder of God's economy. Would you say you have grown in your spiritual, professional and personal life in the last year? If the answer is yes, GREAT! If the answer is no, then let's work on getting you to begin the growth process so that true transformation can begin in you. Remember it is about the power that works within us! Once the growth starts, you are well on your way to seeing the victory over your current situation. Here are a few suggestions to get you started.

1.) **Spiritually** – Ask God to help you pick one area of your life that needs improvement over the next 30 days and then work toward that goal. Make it a point to seek his guidance and to improve your communication skills with the one who can make all the difference in every area of your life. In other words, start talking to God more often. He really does want to listen and speak to you.
2.) **Personally** – In order for you to see radical change and

improvement in the other areas of your life you must also grow in your personal life. You must be on a continual mission to increase your abilities on a personal level. Try to have at least one area of your life that you are "working" on at all times. Maybe this is your ability to communicate with others. Perhaps it is learning to show a little more kindness each day. It could be something as simple as making time for things that you enjoy. Whatever it is that makes you a better person, learn to experience this on a more continual basis. Learn to really live your life to its fullest. Have fun! Enjoy!

3.) **Professionally** - Once you have established yourself in a career path try to be in a state of perpetual learning. This is how you can become an expert at whatever it is that you have chosen to do. Study. Find a mentor. Learn your competition as well as you know yourself. Become the master of your particular field. Once you are walking in your Divine destiny then you have entered the area of your greatest dominion and authority. Learn to exercise that authority over your professional career and you will see the miracle growth and transformation within your own marketplace. Not long ago I was praying over a particular business deal that I had been working on. I remember saying to the Lord, "God, what is it that I am doing wrong? Why can't I seem to get ahead in this particular area?

Why can't I see the change in my marketplace that I need? His answer was simple. **"IF YOU WANT TO CHANGE YOUR MARKETPLACE YOU'VE GOT TO CHANGE WHAT YOU ARE TAKING TO THE MARKET!"** Translation - I hadn't made any adjustments to my marketing message in a long time. It was time for a change. A little adjustment in my message to the market made all the difference in the world. What about you? Have you changed any at all in the past year? Are you still delivering the same "pitch" year after year? Are you still taking the same message to the same people expecting them to react differently? Remember, God is all about increase. How much have you increased lately? Do you think it's time for a change?

Business/Wealth

By now I hope you realize how much God wants to be involved in your business area (and every other area) of your life. For those of you who have been involved in the church realm for any length of time at all, it is probably safe to assume that you have heard some type of "prosperity" message preached. Most of these sermons concentrate largely on the fact that there are treasures laid up in Heaven that God wants to "pour" out on His children. While I do in fact believe that He indeed wants to bless us, I equally believe that there are specific activities that we must do in order to properly prepare and ready ourselves for the wealth and expansion within our businesses and personal lives that true transformation will bring. **With great wealth comes great responsibility and accountability.** Until we live our lives totally under His control regarding our finances, then we will only taste small victories along the way. However, once God knows He can trust us as a conduit for His provision throughout His kingdom, then hold on for the blessings that are bound to come. Just remember, God can only bless you to the extent in which you have prepared for the blessing. He will not put you in a place that may compromise your belief and value system if your core nature has not been totally submitted to the transforming power of Jesus Christ. So, let me ask you a question. What are you doing right now that will prepare you for the blessing spiritually, emotionally, physically and intellectually? You may wonder what I mean. Well, let's look at one example of an outpouring of a blessing for those who weren't ready for all it could bring. Since you may be one of the individuals that is still reading at this point hoping for your first miracle within your marketplace endeavors, I thought it would be interesting to start with the first miracle that Jesus performed publicly. Now let me set the stage for you. Here is a man, known as a carpenter that is attending a wedding where his mother was also present. The story is found in John Chapter Two. It seems that Jesus and his disciples were all invited to the wedding. Picture this, here is Jesus hanging with his disciples at a wedding. Perhaps he was mingling through the crowd or stopping to chat with the bride and groom. Who knows? However, as the story progresses the details begin to take shape. Somewhere in the middle of this festive occasion the host ran out of wine. Apparently the rules of etiquette during this time period where about the same as they are now. It is really not cool for the host to run out of food or drink while throwing a party. But, this is where the story gets interesting. As soon as Mary, the mother of Jesus, hears of this dilemma she makes a straight path over to her son. I can almost see her now pulling him aside so as not to bring embarrassment to anyone, and whispering in his ear. The New King James Version in John 2:3 says, **"And when they ran out of wine, the mother of Jesus said to him, "They have no wine."**

Perhaps it's my twisted sense of humor but I can almost see Jesus looking back at her and leaning in to say, "And why are you telling me this?" (Ok, I have two wonderful boys and I can imagine that this might be their thought given the same circumstance). However, in the 4th verse of the same chapter we find his reply, **"…Woman, what does your concern have to do with Me? My hour has not yet come."** It was His own respectful way of letting his Mom down easy. He wanted her to know that in His mind he wasn't ready to launch his destiny on a group of wedding guests who were obviously very heavy drinkers. ☺ (Just kidding) I mean after all, don't you think His first miracle should have been raising the dead, casting out a demon, or shifting the polar axis or something?

Stop right now, and let's compare notes to what you may be feeling within your company at the moment. Profits are down. The bank has been breathing down your neck about cash flow for over 30 days. If you don't get a miracle soon then it may be hard to cover payroll next week. But, you look around and sadly realize that since you've never really committed the business to the Lord in the first place it might seem a bit greedy to ask for His help now. And why should He help you anyway? Look, there's Bill in shipping. His wife was just diagnosed with cancer and you are worried about slow profits for one month. Or, what about that lady in accounting, Glenda? You just found out that her husband left her and now she has become one of the single Mom statistics that you read about every day. You can almost feel the exhaustion as you pass her in the hallway every morning. You would love to give her a raise to ease some of her financial pressure but you have financial pressure of your own. What gives you the right to ask God for anything anyway? Don't these people need a miracle more than you? And for every Bill and Glenda you can look out over the masses of your employees, customers and vendors and tell thousands of stories just like those.

At what point is it not greed to believe that God could take time away from these hurting people to care enough about your lagging profits to reach out and bring a change in your environment? Maybe it's just not time yet. Maybe this isn't the circumstance in which you should try to launch your newfound interest in a marketplace transformation. Maybe, you should try one more time, this month, to make something happen on your own and forget about asking for any help from above. You keep hearing a little voice in your ear saying, "Come on you can't be seriously thinking that God cares about your business, can you?" Maybe the voice is right. Now, stop again and let's look at it from God's perspective.

Remember, Jesus has just told his Mom that it wasn't time for him to expose His full glory or potential to the public yet. So, in His mind at that very moment a miracle was not on His agenda. But, thank God for Moms who see the unrecognized potential within their children. Based on our previous lesson let's all assume that Jesus was standing on the rung of unrecognized potential with all of the rest of us who get up every single day and report for duty. For each of us there will come that moment in time when we will be asked (or forced) to take a leap of faith to exit that rung so that we may move up the ladder of success. In those times it may take a gentle push from someone to remind us that they "believe" in us. With that belief we can find the inner strength to reach down within ourselves and begin to literally pull out the giftings within us to propel us to the next level within our spiritual and professional walk. This was that moment for Jesus. His Mom knew that He could change the situation. She knew His abilities, and she knew that He was ready. (Moms are good about that sort of thing by the way). She was so confident that He could perform the needed miracle that she told the servants to do whatever it was He told them to do. Now, that is faith. She not only knew He ***could*** do it. She now believed He ***would*** do it. Some of you need to make that same transitional mind set change within yourselves as well. You have always known that God *could* help you. Now, you must believe that He *WILL* help you. Are you ready to see the transformation in your workplace begin? Then ask.

In my mind, I believe that the transition of His Mom's thinking from *could* to *would* is what made the difference. So picture it, Mary had the servants believing now and Jesus was poised and pushed to perform. How do we know this? Because it wasn't very long before Jesus noticed some water pots (six to be exact) that were already sitting on the sidelines in the process of purification. (what are the odds?) Now this was so cool when I read this. Do you get it? The answer was staring all of them in the face. The very things that were needed for this miracle to take place where there and in the "process of purification".

Look around you right now. Do you feel like you have been in the process of purification? Have you been through the fire lately? Has your business been suffering loss or lack of direction? Have you completely run out of ideas? Do you feel like you have nothing left to give? As you look at your employees do you get the feeling that they feel the same way? Well now, isn't that a perfect time for a miracle to happen? Remember, the pots were already at the wedding. They were just empty at the moment and definitely in the category of unrecognized potential. So, to everyone else it may have looked like the party was over. But, with God, unrecognized potential that has been sitting in a holding pattern in "the process of purification", a miracle has been in the making and just waiting to begin. How cool is that?

Are you getting excited yet? So, your mind has probably already gone ahead of me but just in case you haven't skipped ahead in the story let's finish it shall we? So, here we are with the six empty pots and no wine. Talk about a stretch of faith. But, by now Jesus was beginning to see the potential that His mom saw as well. Can't you picture it? He looked around at the guests. Apparently he knew the bride and groom personally to have been invited to the wedding. He knew that it would have been a great embarrassment for them to run out of party favors.

He felt something stirring within Him every time His mom looked over at Him with that look. You know that look. The look that says, well, do something. He takes one final glance at His mom and then back at the servants and the pots. Hey, this might just work! He goes over to the servants and tells them to fill the pots with water. Remember our study earlier on the power of the spoken word?

He gave a command. The servants obeyed without question. After all, who wanted to cross this guy's Mom anyway? So, they not only put a little water in, they filled all of the pots totally up to the brim. There are those moments when you have to give it all you've got. Take a chance and throw caution to the wind. Are you in one of those moments now? Look around you, what do you see? The comedian in me wants to ask you if all you see is a bunch of crackpots. Ok, sorry, I couldn't help it. I guarantee you that you have something, or someone that has been in the process of refining that is ready right now to be your conduit for a miracle. Keep your eyes open and your heart focused on hearing the voice of the Lord. He has the ability to take something **ordinary** and perform a great miracle.

Ok, now the pots have been filled to the brim with water just as Jesus commanded. No doubt, if anyone in the crowd was following this little ordeal they must have been snickering to themselves. They probably thought, oh well, what else is there to do? Perhaps, no one will notice that it's just water. But, it was that final command that made all the difference. It was the power of those words that set the faith in action that brought about the change.

For you see my friend, this time when Jesus spoke, He had transformed ***HIMSELF*** in the matter of a few moments. He went from a man who thought that "it wasn't his time yet" to a man who knew that His words would bring about the transformation in that water that was needed. At that moment, He knew that nothing would ever be the same for Him again. He put His reputation on the line. He put His whole persona and His belief system to the test.

John 2: 8 says, **"And He said to them, "Draw some out now, and take it to the master of the feast."** Why was this important? Think about it for just a minute. By now, the news has probably spread throughout many of the wedding guests. Hey, there's a dude over there who's had a little too much to drink obviously. After all, he has put a bunch of water into some empty pots and is now going to try to turn it into wine and take it to the master of the feast. What an idiot. Does he really think that no one will know the difference between water and wine? If Jesus didn't pull this miracle off then He knew it would be a long time before anyone believed He was the Son of God, if ever. How would you be feeling about right now? Think about it.

What if it was your new idea to "save" the dying profits that was now totally exposed to every employee in the company? All eyes are now on you to see what will happen. They are just waiting on the verdict from the CEO. They can picture you being laughed right out of the company. (Inwardly, you too have thought about that possibility as well) But, you know that you heard the voice of God clearly with that one idea that would make such a drastic change. After all, you used things that were already in your company. The two genius guys in marketing that you found were in the "purification process" with you all along. They had taken every hit with you so far. Together, you came up with that idea that is just about to be presented before the whole company. You can feel your heart pounding out of your chest. What were you thinking? Maybe this wasn't the time to try something new. Maybe it's not your time to move into your glory anyway. Can you sink any further to the back of the room? Or, are you thinking, God you gave us this idea, now take it and breathe life to it and bless this company.

Fast-forward now a bit in the wedding process. Let's read the account in John 2: 8-11.

> **"When the master of the feast had tasted the water that was made wine, and did not know where it came from (but the servants who had drawn the**

> **water knew), the master of the feast called the bridegroom. And he said to him, "Every man at the beginning sets out the good wine, and when the guests have well drunk, then the inferior. You have kept the good wine until now!**
> **This beginning of signs Jesus did in Cana of Galilee, and manifested His glory and His disciples believed in Him."**

There will come a moment for all of us that God will require us to step out in faith to cross over the rung of unrecognized potential and into the realm of blessings and wealth. This will require that you fully understand that God really does want to bless you and that He is keenly aware of what it takes to operate within a professional career or business.

You must realize that Jesus understands business, how it should operate and what it takes to build a successful team. He in fact formed his own team with professionals that had expertise in tax collecting, fishing, medicine and other business endeavors. When he first began his own "ministry" people still referred to him as the carpenter or the carpenter's son. He was known by his profession first.

As we begin to understand our purpose in the workforce we must explore the meaning of transformation. God will use us to bring this transformation, and provide financial support and business expertise to the Kingdom of God. But, what is transformation? According to the definition recorded in Webster's dictionary transformation means **<u>a change in nature or character.</u>** We must be willing to bring the nature and characteristics of God to every place we influence within our workplace and surrounding areas. Can people that work around you really see that you are any different from them? Do they recognize a difference in your character as opposed to their own?

We must be willing to allow the redeeming power of our relationship with the Holy Spirit to work a change within us on a daily basis. If you let Him, God will gently nudge you each time you cross a line that will require an adjustment on your part to further refine His character within you. Let me give you a personal example of His gentle nudging. I work in a very high pace sales environment that often times carries with it very high emotional stress. The company that I work for provides infrastructure cabling and technology to new construction sites as well as existing facilities. There are constant schedule changes and "emergency" activities that occur in the process of any construction related endeavor. At times, any delays could conceivably cost our customers thousands of dollars for every minute that their communications are interrupted. Ok, you get the picture. Stress is the nature of the beast.

On one particular day the stress was getting to me more than normal. I was speaking to one of our project managers over the phone and for a brief moment took out my frustration on him by lowering the boom on him and berating him as if it was his fault (which it wasn't). What I didn't realize at the time was that he had his phone on speakerphone (I do hate that feature). The entire section of the office heard me hollering into the phone. Now, I could justify it by saying that at least I didn't use any foul language but that would be a poor attempt to hide the truth. The truth is that I messed up. It wasn't this poor guy's fault that our schedule wasn't met. In fact, he was really my favorite Project Manager. I can't really explain what tipped the scales of insanity over for me that day but the deed was done. It didn't take more than a millisecond for the Lord to speak to me to tell me I had to go apologize to him. Ok. No problem. I knew that I owed him that.

However, it was the second part of the instruction that was a bit harder to swallow. God also told me that I had to apologize to him privately as well as publicly. Ok, I was thinking that I would go over to that section of the office (about 10 or so people) and publicly apologize for my behavior and humble myself before them. But, even that was not all the Lord required. Remember, in order to bring true transformation there must be a difference within our character that can be seen as totally and radically different from anything else your co-workers have ever experienced. In order to fully walk into your true destiny you will be required to purge every ounce of ego or self-reliance from your system. You must be willing to expose your weaknesses so that others will understand that you have submitted to a higher authority that now has control of your actions. Well, to finish my story. The Lord instructed me that since I had my "outburst" over a speakerphone for all to hear then I had to perform my apology across the public address system of our entire company. I did put up a bit of a fight. My argument to God was that I only had about 10 people who even knew this little incident had occurred. If I gone over the PA system then, the entire company, as well as our assembly and shipping departments, would hear me begging for forgiveness.

However, I have learned that with God when He gives an instruction He expects it to be carried out. See, it wasn't just about me anymore. It was about the poor man that I had taken out the frustration of the day on. I had unintentionally hurt his feelings publicly for all to hear. He was a good man and didn't deserve my tirade. It was also about my claim to be a "Christian". It was now about embarrassing God as well. So, I knew I couldn't put off the inevitable. When God gives you an instruction; just do it. He has a greater purpose in mind. So, I immediately (within 10 minutes of the outburst) got on our PA system and apologized for my behavior to the poor guy. I admitted that I was a jerk and let the words, "I was wrong" ring through the entire company. At that moment it seemed that my every word was being magnified 1000 times and that it echoed through every office, corridor, and hallway. In my mind at that moment, I could picture it flooding all the way to space (Okay, I have a great imagination). Well, you try apologizing over a PA system sometime and see how insignificant you feel. Anyway, as soon as I did that, not only did I feel an immediate freedom and release, but this man came and gave me the biggest bear hug. This meant the world to him. He said I didn't have to do it. But, you see, I did. I had to do it because God was teaching me a lesson. Other people are just as important as we are and have just as an important place in our lives and in the Kingdom of God. To this day, this guy is loyal to me and I to him. We formed a bond that day that has lasted many years. From that moment on, he knew that I cared enough to admit when I was wrong. I learned that God would require of us a deeper understanding of our own character as we attempt to develop His character within our hearts and lives.

Has God been speaking to you lately about anything that he wants you to do at work to correct any wrong behavior? Until you deal with His last instruction you will not be able to move ahead to the next level. Ok, I can't be the only one that royally messes up can I? Some of you have been sitting on an instruction for a while. May I humbly suggest that you get it done? Then you can move to the next level.

Kings

Now, here we go to the meat of the principles within God's economy. What is the definition of a King and what is their purpose? First, let's take a look at Revelation 1:6 in the New King James Version. It says,

> **"And has made us kings and priests to His God and Father, to Him be glory and dominion forever and ever. Amen"**

Since Marketplace Ministry has gained more and more focus as of late many of you may already have heard the terms Kings and Priests thrown around in conversations. For purposes of making this simple, the definition of a King as far as Marketplace endeavors are concerned is this. The King is the one who provides the provision (money) to allow for Kingdom expansion and who operates under the covering of a priest. Many times it is the King who will fund the vision of the priest. We will talk about the role of the priest in detail a bit later in this chapter. People are looking for a King to lead them. 1 Samuel 8:5 says,

> **"Now make us a king to judge us like all the Nations."**

In the business world there will always be a need for someone to take the lead and develop a business strategy that will magnify God and promote His kingdom principles. God is looking for someone who will be willing to stand with ethics and integrity in the business decisions that are made on a daily basis. Let's face it, most people want all the glory but don't want to take the heat of having to be the one to make the tough decisions that often times fall squarely on the shoulders of those in leadership. For each of us who have been called to operate under the mantle of a King, God will give us the vision and focus that our particular kingdom is to concentrate on. The Principles of Kingship will be covered in the pages that follow.

Priests

A Priest is one who is anointed by God to establish the corporate vision for the body of Christ either locally, or elsewhere, that he has been appointed and ordained to represent and cover. He is the one that ministers to all of those within the church walls as well as to those in the world. As the priest seeks the Lord for a strategy and plan to bring transformation to the city to which they have been assigned, many times the partnership and support of a King is essential for the provision to be equal to that of the call. In the Old Testament we learn that the Kings are the ones who supported the priest and brought the provision into the tabernacle for the complete support of the ministries represented. This union between Priest and King was one of the strongest bonds recorded. As long as that fellowship remained and the two walked within their particular anointing, the Hand of the Lord was shown in miraculous ways to all the enemies of the Lord.

Unfortunately, many priests today do not truly understand the divine partnership and relationship that should be present by joining these two realms. Each truly needs the other. However, many Pastors today feel inadequate to understand or "speak" into the lives of the Kings within their congregation. Many of these Kings have risen to unbelievable power and respect within their spheres of influence and this can become intimidating for any Pastor. However, Pastor, may I speak to you as a King right now from my heart and tell you a little secret? We are not asking you to give us our next business plan or to somehow prophetically tell us what our next vertical market move should entail. All we are asking is that as we submit ourselves to your covering and to the leadership of the Lord, that you will hold our name and our business up in prayer. We humbly ask that you respect our time and our talents as much as you would respect some well-known "minister of the gospel". We simply ask that you care enough about all attributes of our life, including our workplace, and that you would commit to spending time to cover us in prayer. And, if by chance you get a word from the Lord for us, please don't hesitate to speak into our lives. We crave your input. We crave your anointing and your covering. We seek your blessing.

One of the greatest Pastors that I have ever had the privilege of working with truly understood the role of the Kings within his congregation. He respected the time of the business people within his congregation. If he called a meeting, he made sure to adhere to the agenda and to the time allotted. He understood that for these men and women, their time was one of the most valuable gifts that they could give. To each of these individuals time represented money. He also understood that these individuals had already set aside a portion of that money and had dedicated it to the advancement of the Kingdom within that city and to those nations around the world that his particular dreams and visions represented. There were many times I would look out my office window only to see my Pastor walking the parking lot. I knew what he was doing. He was helping me cover that business in prayer and also covering me and my efforts. Most of the time he never even knew that I saw him out there. Just knowing that he was praying made those contract negations go much smoother! You may think that this seems a bit too far out for you to comprehend. However, this Pastor got it. He understood the principles of the Priests and Kings anointing. He knew that the more my business and personal life was blessed, the more "provision" would be added to the ministry endeavors of his vision for the city. **We were a team working hand-in-hand for one purpose.** That purpose was to see the transformation of our city by the difference that an encounter with Jesus Christ can bring.

Pastors, may I ask you a question? Do you know the business people within your congregation? When was the last time that you or one of your staff called and offered a prayer or better yet went to that person's place of business and spent time in prayer for them? Have you ever done it? If not, may I encourage you to do so? The results will be far beyond your comprehension. If you truly want to do more for the Kingdom then you are going to need the provision to do it. Short of money falling directly down from Heaven above, it will take a myriad of people in the marketplace being blessed in their efforts and then taught to continuously keep filling the storehouse. Trust me when I tell you that they are waiting for you. They are praying for someone right now to come alongside their business endeavors and to pray for them and cover them. If you don't do it, God will send someone else who will.

At present, I am personally covering quite a few businesses and particular career paths of a few because they couldn't find a Pastor who was willing to come to their business or to speak into their professional life. I did not ask for this role but will gladly fill it until someone else is willing to share the load. May I respectfully submit that it is foolish to think that you can ask for their provision without ever having shared in their marketplace journey? Sadly, this is a common occurrence. Often times it is left to other Kings to cover the activities of their fellow workplace warriors. If your ministry is struggling financially I strongly urge you to consider praying over the business affairs of your congregation. The provision you so desperately need is probably already within your reach.

I know that this is not true of every Pastor, but if you abdicate the position to which you have been assigned then how can you get the provision you need? Chances are that an "uncovered" King will ask another "King" to cover them in prayer. Why? Because, as a King, I understand the dilemma that another King faces intimately. I understand the pressure to sacrifice values at the altar of success. I understand that what worked before isn't working anymore. I understand the pressure to produce more profits and more revenue where none exists.

As a manager I sometimes feel as if the struggle to stay ahead of the competition is choking the very life force out of most employees. All of us now work the equivalence of three jobs and must maintain this pace if we are to stay employed. Is it any wonder that as you look out over your congregation on Sunday morning that they look exhausted? They have spent the entire week trying desperately to succeed in their job without sacrificing their ethics, morals, values, family and Christianity. It may sound easy, but I assure you that on some days it takes every ounce of strength to reach down into the depths of your soul and pull out of your spiritual reserve to stay the course.

While others compromise their convictions to make their quota there are those who refuse to bow to the demands of mainstream corporate propaganda. They have drawn their line in the sand and stand firmly with their banner held high. At times, they feel alone, and frankly used. Mainstream corporations think nothing of eliminating them for the sake of salvaging overhead. For many, they are just a number. Please, don't let them feel that way in the sanctity of your flock as well. They need a safe harbor to anchor and gain refreshment and rejuvenation for the boardroom wars and competitive cutthroats that are in their future. Now, do you get a glimpse as to why they need extra prayer? Do you see why they seem to gaze at you with pleading eyes? Let me interpret that look for you. It is one that I am sure I have portrayed at one time or another throughout my spiritual journey. It is a look from someone who would like to hear that you are praying for them. (I mean really praying for them) The look simply says, "Pastor, I need you more than you realize. Please, help me."

For those who have called and begged for prayer, I have gone as a King and a Priest to anoint their business and lay my hands on them and pray for them. I encouraged them to seek a Pastor that would embrace their business endeavors and speak into their life. Pastors, once more, let me encourage you to rise to the challenge of those of us who call ourselves a King. At times we may be like trying to hold a ring of fire, but as you pray for us, cover us, mentor us, and correct us, you will be able to partner together as we set the world on fire for the Kingdom! Kings need a Pastor!

So, to sum up this little section on God's economy we have covered quite a bit. We learned that all of us start out as unrecognized potential just waiting for us to step out in faith and launch our marketplace careers. As we use our faith within our sphere of influence God brings wealth and blessing to our business affairs. As we exercise this authority within our life we truly walk into the mantle of a marketplace King. As a King we know that the blessings bestowed upon us are also meant as a provision for the Kingdom of God. To that end, we need to submit to a Priest to whom God has joined our hearts and provide for his vision and ask for his covering in prayer.

As we get all avenues of our life together within the economy of God, then we can rest assured that we have really reached a point in our lives where our destiny within the Kingdom of God has been found. **When we operate in the anointing and gifting to which we have been called, then our economy will never be controlled by natural market projections**. As we are fulfilling the will of God, His economy will ensure that we have the provision needed for each day and to supply the vision. In God's economy the law of blessing and provision is always available to those who commit their marketplace walk to Him. God's economy is the safest investment you will ever make!

FIFTH LESSON: I MUST MOVE PAST THE RUNG OF UNRECOGNIZED POTENTIAL IF I AM TO WALK INTO THE TRUE WEALTH GOD INTENDED FOR ME WITHIN MY PROFESSIONAL CAREER.

Questions to consider:

1.) Do you fully understand the principles of God's economy?
2.) Have you moved past your unrecognized potential and started bearing fruit in your marketplace?
3.) Have you sought the covering of a Pastor over your business endeavors?
4.) Are you ready to provide money into the kingdom and embrace the vision to transform your city for Christ?

Chapter Six - The Principle of Foundation

Well, we have spent quite a bit of time thus far just setting up the basic parameters of marketplace understanding. However, as we move forward, let's really examine in detail the great plan that God has for a King and what His requirements for blessing entail. It is in this stage of our journey that you will understand ***The Principle of Foundation***. The more you understand the foundation of your kingdom and all the elements that operate within your realm, the smoother and easier your life will become. The attention and detail that you show to your kingdom in the beginning, will directly affect the amount of success you achieve and the amount of stress and sorrow you avoid. Although there are no true pat answers or easy formulas as some would have you believe, ***The Principle of Foundation,*** will help you in your thought processes regarding your anointing and in planning for your kingdom.

Sorry to break this to you, but there are no easy lotto numbers on this one. The road of a King requires dedication, perseverance, commitment, obedience, at times a sense of humor and a willingness to be a completely pliable vessel in the hands of the Master. There will be bumps along the road as you seek to grow your kingdom. However, if you are willing, then He is able! He wants to inject Himself into your marketplace endeavors. Since you asked Him to help you when we first got started I think it's safe to assume that we are now on our way to walking this kingly journey together. So, hang on. Here we go! May God truly bless everything you put your hand to, from this time forward. May you know which deals to pursue and which ones to let die. May the discernment that you need for every transaction flood through you on a daily basis. May your efforts be blessed as you commit your resources to the Kingdom of God! Are you assigned as a King?

> **"We, however, will not boast beyond proper limits, but will confine our boasting to the field God has assigned to us, a field that reaches even to you." (2 Corinthians 10:13)**

If you answered yes, then your field of influence is the marketplace. It is outside the walls of the church. So, hopefully by the time we finish our journey together you will have confidence that God placed you exactly where He wanted you. He knew that only you could reach some of the people that you will meet along your way. If He placed you there, then rest in the fact that you are fully equipped to fulfill your calling. You are not out there alone, (even though at times you may feel that way). You are there with the authority and power of the King of all Kings. Get it settled in your mind once and for all that you are just as anointed as anyone else. Believe me, when you are in the heat of the battle, trying to win a multi-million dollar contract against some very stiff competition, you better know you are anointed!

So let's get started chatting about the characteristics of a King and ***The Principle of Foundation***. As with anything there are certain rules and parameters that govern proper behavior. They are the rules of engagement so to speak. This is true of every occupation, and being a King is no different. In fact, God has specific guidelines for you that you must follow if you want to walk into your full potential. Let's first look at what elements are in your kingdom, shall we? I think that will help solidify in your mind all the details within your kingdom. After all, if you are a King, then you have a kingdom. Within your kingdom you will have the following represented.

- **God**
- **God's vision for the king or his business**
- **The king's trusted advisors**
- **Those who are willing to serve under your leadership**

Now, let's look at each of these individually.

God

Well, this is a given. If we are totally committed to allow God free reign and access into our marketplace, then He must be present. He will be there to give us our assignment and provide the details and instructions that we must follow if we are to fulfill our destiny. God will be the ultimate covering that will overshadow, direct, and protect our investments within our sphere of influence. One of the greatest lessons that the Lord has taught me is how important it is to stay in a continual state of seeking His presence. This is the only way to ensure that our actions remain pure and focused on Kingdom advancement.

God's Vision for the King and His Business

A King will be blessed by God and given strategies to put in place as he fights the battle for his workplace. As a king seeks the Lord for guidance, then the daily activities of his business will adopt an entirely different mindset. A king must pray for the mind of Christ to be evident in his or her life. When the mind of Christ rules, then wisdom and discernment will follow. These two things are vital if you are to survive the jungle that we call work.

In the business world there will always be a need for someone to take the lead and develop a business strategy that will magnify God and promote His kingdom principles. God is looking for someone who will be willing to stand with ethics and integrity in the business decisions that are made on a daily basis.

1) How do you react when someone cheats you out of a deal?

2) How do you treat your employees?
3) How do you treat you boss?
4) Do you seek God's counsel as you approach new business deals?
5) Do you ask God to give you strategies for your business?

It is important to remember that almost every kingdom throughout history has been established by war. Kings must be willing to go to war and fight for the vision that God has placed within them. The war may be physical, emotional, or spiritual. This is why the Word of God spends time addressing the weapons of our warfare. Kings rule by **inheritance** or **conquest**! There may be those of you who were blessed enough to have a business handed to you. If that is the case then you rule by *inheritance.* Sometimes these kingdoms are the hardest to maintain. Why? The answer is simple. You didn't do anything to establish yourself as the rightful owner of that kingdom. It was given to you. To put it bluntly, you have no skin in the game up to this point. However, never forget that there are always those seeking to overthrow every kingdom. History has proven time and again that rule by inheritance doesn't guarantee success. But, if you want to keep what has been entrusted to you then you must learn to fight. Some in the business world refer to it as the art of war. Once again God directed us through His word and is way ahead of the 'cultural gimmicks" of current business acumen. Even King David commented while praying one day that it was God who taught his hands to war. Do you want to keep your Kingdom? Learn to fight. Learn to strategize. It's tough out in the trenches, so trust me when I tell you that you will need His help to wage the war against rising costs, lower profits, and stiff competition. You will need Him to teach your hands to war to keep your inheritance.

For those of us who didn't inherent any business we are left to find our kingdoms by conquest. Now that's what I'm talking about! For those of us who embrace a challenge, we find this the most exciting. To establish a kingdom through this method takes a lot of prayer, patience, resolve, wisdom and downright intervention from Heaven. Most of the time it is not an overnight success story. Rather, it is one of determination, stamina and faith. In this particular scenario you find yourself out there in the muddy waters of commerce trying to find your place of dominance and destiny along with the rest of the masses. For some this happens quickly. For others, it may take a lifetime of commitment. Either way, war is inevitable. So whether you inherited the kingdom or you are taking it by force, the truth is that you still will have to fight. At some point in the game, you will have to roll up your sleeves, grit your teeth, dig in your heels and determine that this will be the day you make your stand for victory. If this is that day for you then congratulations! So, let's get our battle minds ready and begin.

The first rule of engagement is to know the enemy. If you are going to *maintain* or *expand* the kingdom that has been entrusted to you then you must recognize the real enemy. Ephesians 6:12 says:

> **"For we do not wrestle against flesh and blood, but against principalities, against powers, against the rulers of the darkness of this age, against spiritual hosts of wickedness in the heavenly places."**

There may be some of you who would like to believe that the enemy is the VP down the hall, or the CEO who doesn't have a clue about what it takes to win a bid in this competitive market. (Give them credit since they are probably fighting their own battles for survival). Perhaps, you think of your competition as the enemy. But, let's face it. The real enemies of our kingdom are the powers and principalities of darkness that are in a full court press to make sure that you don't make your quota or that the bottom line keeps getting thinner and thinner. Why? The enemy knows if he can defeat you on your turf (your marketplace), then he has won in the battle of your mind. If your mind begins to doubt (even a little) then your kingdom can come crumbling around you quickly. Without you, and the provision that your kingdom provides, the enemy knows that the vision of the Priest can literally be halted overnight. That is why it is critical that you stay fully alert and ready to fight for everything within your business and professional career. The provision for growth within the Kingdom of God is coming from **<u>YOU</u>**!

Now, remember we are still talking about ***The Principle of Foundation***. We are still learning the principles that will guide our kingdom to victory. Up to this point we have learned that God must be at the core of our business endeavors. We have also learned that no matter how a kingdom was originally established it is certain that in order to maintain it we must learn to fight. A kingdom requires war! Now, let's learn about the armor according to Ephesians 6:13-18.

Verse 13 – **"Therefore take up the whole armor of God, that you may be able to withstand in the evil day, and having done all, to stand."**

First, before you go out to battle you must understand that you have to take the WHOLE armor of God to be effective. Picture it like this. Would you go out of your house only partially dressed? Sadly, many of us don't equip ourselves properly before going out to the war we face everyday in the marketplace. This verse should be one of the most encouraging verses in scripture for those of us who are out there in the daily fight. Why? Because, it promises that if we use the whole armor of God, then we will be able to withstand in the evil day and KEEP standing. In other words, we won't be knocked down. We will still be standing. At the end of the day isn't that what most of us want? We want to still be standing! What a great comfort.

Verse 14-15 – **"Stand therefore, having girded your waist with truth, having put on the breastplate of righteousness, and having shod your feet with the preparation of the gospel of peace."**

Are you still with me? If you are, then you have decided to get totally dressed in God's armor before going out to work anymore. Way to go! (I'm sure the neighbors will be happy!) ☺

Ok, stay with me. If our Kingdom is dedicated to God, then there will be some requirements for blessing. Sorry, but nothing is ever easy is it? The first requirement for victory in the battle is truth. Now we could spend an entire book on this subject. If you are going to represent God in the marketplace it is critical that you be known for truth.

How many times have you made "little" compromises thinking it didn't really matter? How many times have you purposely left something out of a proposal document or "hidden" some fees into a vague scope of work just so you could edge out a bit more profit? How many times have you misrepresented yourself or your company just to get the deal? If you are the owner of the company how many times have you made a promise or commitment to an employee or customer but then failed to follow through? If you don't start your business, or business transaction with truth then you might as well hang it up now. You must walk in truth if you are seeking God's blessing on your business.

Did you ever wonder why truth is around our waist as part of our armor? Your waist is your core. When you use the armor of God then truth is what establishes the core of your business. What's at your core right now? If it's not truth, then you need to have a chat with the Lord and ask for His forgiveness and His help.

You must also have on the breastplate of righteousness. The breastplate could be considered the attributes that go out before us. With that in mind, what is righteousness? It is our code of ethics and moral behavior. It is the part of our character that ensures that we do that right thing *every time*. What code of ethics do you follow in your professional life? What are you known for? Do you find yourself ever crossing the line? Do you ever find yourself thinking about situational ethics? Well, just this once, in this circumstance, maybe it will be ok if I let this one little thing slide.

If you take off your breastplate even once, thinking that it doesn't matter or that no one is looking, you have just compromised your wardrobe. You have left the designer label of Heaven to don the bargain shopper's threads. Translation? You took off part of your holy clothes. In order to ensure victory you must have the WHOLE armor of God on at all times! Do people refer to you as someone who is righteous? Think about it.

Now, as any good fashion guru knows we can't leave out the shoes! Ok, guys, humor me here for a minute. According to the scripture we must have our feet covered in the preparation of the gospel of peace. There are two very clear messages in these passages for those of us in the marketplace. First, don't go out to war without the proper preparation. How many times have you thrown a presentation together knowing that it could have been better? How many times have you gone to a meeting unprepared and then wondered why there seemed to be conflict? If you are going out to war, then go prepared. Second, go with the gospel of peace.

Ok, I am the first to admit that this one is the tough part for me. There are times I would love to blast into a meeting and give all of them a nice tongue-lashing. But remember, according to the fashion etiquette rules of the Kingdom I need to walk in the gospel of peace. Boy, will that make you think the next time you feel your blood pressure rising in the middle of a meeting. If we are to represent Christ in the marketplace then we must be ambassadors of peace.

Now to finish off our heavenly attire let's examine verses 16-17 in Ephesians chapter six.

> **"above all, taking the shield of faith with which you will be able to quench all the fiery darts of the wicked one. And take the helmet of salvation, and the sword of the Spirit, which is the word of God."**

Ok, now we are getting down to the good part! It's time for us to take out the shield of faith. In the business arena this can sometimes be our hardest challenge. Talk about calling those things that are not as though they were! It takes faith to get up every day and believe that you can become the "rain man (or woman)" for your company. In other words, it takes faith to know and proclaim that your territory is expanding as your kingdom grows. Since this has been a building process just remember that all other areas of our life need to be in line for our faith to be able to produce the desired result. Once our life is fully committed to the Lord, then our faith can call into action the very things that are needed within our professional lives.

Do you need more business? Faith can bring it in. Do you need more revenues? Faith can bring them in. Do you need additional market segments to be opened for you? Faith can open those doors for you. Do you know what else faith can do for you? It is through faith that you will be able to put out all those nagging little fires that your enemy (competition) will throw your way. You know the ones I mean. The little distractions that become the things that haunt you in the middle of the night. Those little "what if" scenarios that keep running through your mind each time you try to get some rest. Use your faith to put a stop to this. Faith is the key to turn the tide for your business.

Finally, take the helmet of salvation (that personal relationship with Jesus Christ) and the sword of the Spirit (the Word of God) and finish off the rest of whatever is left of your enemy. The chapter concludes by instructing us to keep praying and watching with perseverance. Why? Well, it is through prayer that we keep our kingdom and guard it against those that may seek to destroy it.

The Principle of Foundation is also important as we seek to fully understand the calling of a King. The parable of the talents is a glimpse into some of the requirements for the blessing of a kingdom. Why? Because remember if you accept this mission of becoming a King for the advancement of the Kingdom, then He will expect you to use your talents and to increase them! Let's look at Matthew 25:14-20 together. It says,

> **"Again, it will be like a man going on a journey who called his servants and entrusted his property to them. To one he gave five talents of money, to another two talents, and to another one talent, each according to his ability. Then he went on his journey.**
> **The man who had received the five talents went at once and put his money to work and gained five more. So also, the one with the two talents gained two more. But the man who had received the one talent went off, dug a hole in the ground and his master's money. After a long time the master of those servants returned and settled accounts with them. The man who had received the five talents brought the other five. "Master", he said, "you entrusted me with five talents. See, I have gained five more."**

One of the first keys you need to understand in your Kingly endeavors is that God distributes "talents" based on ability. Some have said that you can basically "claim" what you want and then it will come to you. But, may I humbly ask you a question? If God gives gifts according to abilities, then how much time do you spend trying to improve on the abilities that you currently have? What or who is your greatest asset? I'll give you a hint. It's you. It's not the company you work for or the products you sell, even though they both may be great.

How much time do you spend on yourself personally, on growing your abilities or making "you" better? If God, as the scripture tells us, gives gifts according to our abilities, then why do you spend much of your time asking for things for which you know in your heart you are not ready? (Ouch) (Sorry about that one). What am I saying? How many people ask to win the lottery but wouldn't have the slightest clue of what to do with it if they got it. He will not give you more than you can handle. This would not be the plan of a loving Father. For someone to tell you otherwise is a great injustice to you and to the kingdom.

How about a practical example? Would you give your 15 year old a brand new Porsche without them ever having been behind a wheel? Would you give $10,000.00 to a man you know had a problem with gambling? Then why would God, in His love and mercy, give us things that we are not ready for or that would hurt us? So, with that in mind, find your gifting and then begin studying so that you are the best at whatever it is you do. If you are in sales, then become a master of the product you are selling. If you are a physician, then become the master of your particular specialty. Study to show yourself ready and approved for the blessings that God has in store for you. Keep it forever at the forefront of your mind and remember that we are trying to lay a proper foundation. We are trying to make sure that your structure is ready to handle the pressure and blessings that will come your way!

Remember our discussion on your purpose? If we are to bring transformation into the marketplace then we not only need to study, but we must also be an able torchbearer for the name of Christ. We must be the example of the true character of Christ shinning in our workplace. We must live by a higher calling. So, when we have those moments when we would simply love to "choke a fellow employee", we must first ask ourselves if that is what Jesus would want us to do. Since the answer to that question is clearly no, we know that we must take the high road so that His name can be protected. Although this is a humorous example, it is meant to gently remind you that once you accept the responsibility of a King, it is no longer about you. It is about the Kingdom of God! For the sake of all who try, if you aren't going to act like a Christian, then don't claim to be one. Please.

What is your reputation in your current marketplace? Are you a good example of Christ where you are placed at the moment?

Not long ago I was having a meeting with an employee from a company that competes with mine. As we were chatting, we began to talk about faith. Even though he is not a Christian, he still dialogues with me about faith almost every time we see each other. At one point in our careers we both worked for a company who's owner claimed to be a Christian. However, when it came to fulfilling the employment agreements that were in our contracts for payment, this person clearly forgot that God is a God who expects us to keep the covenants we make with our employees, our family and friends, and Him. In fact, I'm fairly certain during these moments that any Christianity was out of the door. (We will talk in depth about covenants in the later chapters). Suffice it to say that God is not happy if we don't keep our word. When we don't obey, the blessing can not come. During my conversation with this fellow employee he made a statement that not only shocked me, but it has stayed with me ever since. In fact it was probably one of the things that first sparked the passion of the marketplace within me. He said, "I will never again work for someone who has a *fish* on the back of their car." Wow!

What a terrible statement and testament about our representation of Christ in the workplace. I asked him right then if I had ever done anything to disgrace the name of Christ. If I had, I wanted to apologize. I didn't want to add my name to those of his long list of "Christians" who had cheated him in some way in business. Please understand that more people than you realize are observing your commitment to Christ in the workplace. They are taking notes I assure you.

Try to remember that as you are representing Christ in your place of employment that He will automatically get the blame for anything you or I do that will be less than perfect. Not to burden you, but you must rise to a higher calling if you are to live the life of a King and fulfill your destiny. You must have a higher degree of ethics and code of conduct than anyone else in the company. You must be the example that He demands. We will study a king's marketplace in depth in a later chapter as we explore deeper into the requirements of blessings in the journey of kingship.

The King's trusted advisors

A King will be blessed by God and given strategies to put in place as he fights the battle for his workplace. As a king seeks the Lord for guidance, then the daily activities of his business will adopt an entirely different mindset. A king must pray for the mind of Christ to be evident in his or her life. When the mind of Christ rules, then all wisdom and discernment will follow.

When you truly turn your professional life and business career over to the leading of the Spirit then take comfort in the fact that God will always place those within your life that can be trusted. They will be your advocates, your advisors, your fellow warriors, and many times some of your dearest friends. He will place within these closest companions those who can hear from Him on behalf of your business. 1 Samuel 10:26 in the Amplified says,

> **"Saul also went home to Gibeah: and there went with him a band of valiant men, whose hearts God had touched."**

Every King needs to surround himself with people who are gifted in areas that they are not. They also need to be able to recognize people that can be trusted implicitly. There are times when God may speak to them before He speaks to you. Be willing to listen and take the appropriate action. It is critical to pay attention to the company you keep.

Do you have anyone that consistently prays over your business or career? If not, you truly need to develop a circle of people that you trust that can speak into your life and pray with you over your marketplace endeavors. These people will become the covering that helps protect you and your kingdom from the attacks of the enemy. There will be times when these individuals that you trust will gently bring you correction regarding your focus. Remember, these are people who have willingly agreed to travel this journey with you. They will be looking out for your best interests and those of your kingdom. They are also there to bring accountability.

All of us need advice, correction, mentoring and coaching. Prayerfully consider the team of advisors in your life. They are there to make sure you stay alive out there in the marketplace. As such, they are vital to your success. Pay attention to every relationship that is brought into your life and guard them carefully. It is this team of people that will stand with you in battle. So, know them well. Once the battle is on, you need to know you can count on them.

Those who are willing to serve under your leadership

God will place people within your circle of fiends that will be willing to serve under your leadership. There will also be those who are called to be your armor bearers. The duty of an armor bearer is to keep the king alive. When you study the lives of the kings in the Old Testament there are the stories of those courageous men called the armor bearers. Many times these were the guys who went before the king in battle to scope out the territory. At the very least they were at the side of their king during every skirmish and every battle. Samuel 14:7 says:

> **"So his armor bearer said to him, "Do all that is in your heart. Go then here I am with you according to your heart"**

God will place people within your company, individuals that will put their full strength behind seeing your company's vision accomplished. He will knit their hearts with yours so there will be strength of purpose and focus. These are the guys and gals that can take a few shots with you. They aren't afraid of heading into battle and confronting the competition with you.

Look around your life at the moment. Who would you say would be the armor bearers in your life right now? Who has been there for you during the good times and the bad times of the company? Who has stood by you during every business transaction whether good or bad? Who are the people that have been most faithful? What employees have stuck with you no matter what the market indicators? Can you name them now? If so, my suggestion would be to guard them with your very life and career. These people have been there for you. These are the loyal faithful who you can trust to be there when the chips are down or when the profits are rolling in. These are rare individuals indeed. Is it your assistant? How about the guy in HR that has been with you since the beginning? What about the woman in AR that has been working extra hours since a company downsizing took most of her staff? How about the vendors who have worked with you when your cash flow made it almost impossible to stay current?

Perhaps it's your spouse that put up with all those late nights, missed dinners and forgotten appointments. Whoever it may be, my suggestion is that you take a moment right now to thank God for them and to personally thank them. When is the last time you shot your armor bearer a note of thanks? They deserve it don't you think? If you are going to keep the foundation of your business solid, you will need them in the future.

To sum up this chapter on the ***Principle of Foundation*** we have learned how important it is to understand the elements that have been placed within your kingdom. All of us have the same elements at our disposal. The difference is what we do with them and how we apply them. Your marketplace endeavors are very important to God. Go back through the lessons we learned in this chapter and jot down some notes and keep track of the people that are your foundational core. You will want to know who they are in the future.

SIXTH LESSON: I CANNOT WALK OUTSIDE OF THE COVERING THAT HIS PRESENCE DEMANDS.

Questions to consider:

1.) Can you list your core belief system in detail?
2.) Have you entrusted your kingdom to the rule of God?
3.) Do you know the vision God has for you?
4.) Do you consider your "spiritual" wardrobe everyday?
5.) Do you know who your most trusted advisors are? Write them down.
6.) Can you personally name those who have agreed to walk the journey with you? When was the last time you thanked them?

Chapter Seven - The Principle of Marketplace Authority

What Brings the Wealth?

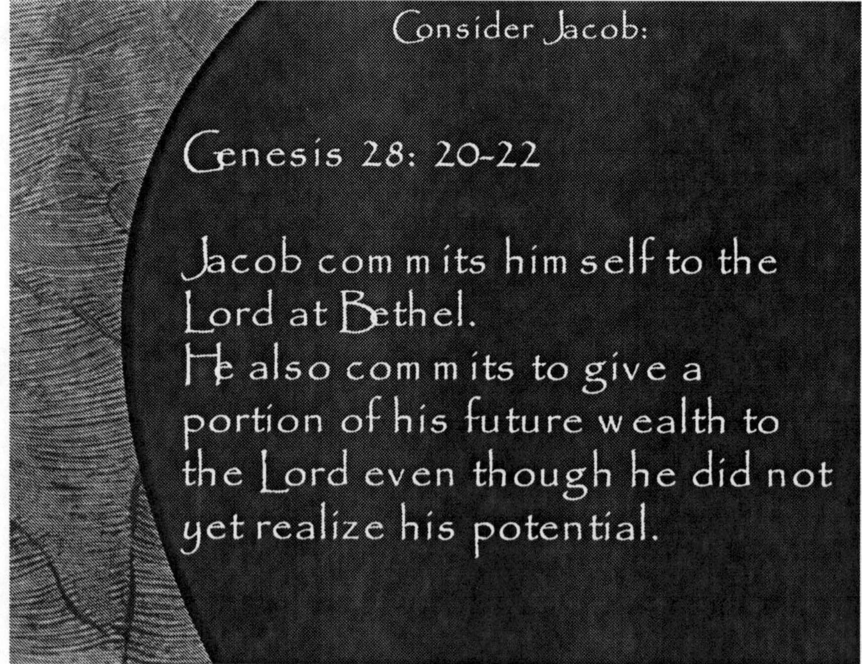

As we begin the in-depth study of the habits of a King I thought it important for us to consider the life of Jacob. As we study his life in depth we will understand ***The Principle of Marketplace Authority***. There are many attributes that God expects before He can trust us with the wealth. If we learn these principles, then we will understand the actions that bring wealth. Until we truly learn these lessons, we will never be able to walk into our full potential. There are standards of accountability that we must follow if we are to walk in the creativity and blessing that God wants for all of us. So, let's explore authority together, shall we?

Jacob began his professional career on a bit of a down note. Well, let's just call it like we see it. He cheated. He stole his brother's birthright (some would blame his mother) and began his company on the run. Literally. He took out running for his life, and landed at his Uncle Laban's house. I'm not sure how your particular company was started but one that is begun on the fly can be a bit of a bear to get a handle on. ☺

Perhaps, you also find yourself in a position where you cheated or lied to get to where you are at this moment. Well, hopefully by now you have asked for forgiveness. If this is the case, there is still hope, so don't be discouraged. If your company is on solid footing as to its foundation then great for you! Your road to success may be a bit easier. But when all is said and done, we all have the same rules to follow and the same expectations of excellence. So, let's dig a little deeper into Jacob and the original foundation of his company and future wealth.

If you have ever had any dealings with any type of construction then you know that the foundation is the most critical part of the structure. It is absolutely essential that we build it to last. After all, the entire weight of the future structure will be resting on that foundation. In terms of building a company, the foundation is just as critical. All of the future success, failures, wins, loses, and everything that will come between in your journey down the path of marketplace leadership will be resting on the core foundational principals that you establish at the beginning. So, let's make sure we get it right. Are you ready?

As we learned a moment ago, Jacob began his corporate life on the run. However, just prior to landing at Laban's, he takes a rest at a place called Bethel. It was at Bethel that he made his vow to God concerning his business and his future riches. I find this very interesting. Although he came from a position of wealth within his own family, as he is praying at Bethel he is flat broke. I mean he has nothing except a stolen birthright. Yet, this man, who by all business accounts is totally busted, spoke to God about his situation. He had enough courage and faith to offer a **plea and a promise**.

Is that where you are today? Do you feel busted in more ways than one? If so, are you ready to offer a plea, a promise, or both? Before you are too quick to answer, think. Jacob promised a portion of his future wealth to God. Ok, it was a plea and a prayer. At some point, if all went well, he knew he would have to pay up. The question at that moment was, **would he**? Would the man who began his company with a lie actually keep his promise? If you were God, what would you have done? Would you have answered this broke, busted, cheating man's plea? Hmmmmm, something to think about isn't it? Let's just pretend for a moment that you were God, and that you decide to extend a second chance. Then, my humble advice to you is pay attention to the vows you make. One day, you will have to pay up! Now let's check out the rest story.

> The New King James Version states in verses 20-22:
>
> **"Then Jacob made a vow, saying, "If God will be with me, and keep me in this way that I am going, and give me bread to eat and clothing to put on, so that I come back to my father's house in peace, then the Lord shall be my God. And this stone which I have set as a pillar shall be God's house, and of all that you give me I will surely give a tenth to you."**

Now, let's take note of a few things. Jacob promises God a

portion of his future wealth as long as he has food to eat and clothes to put on. You may think, yeah well given the circumstances I would have done the same thing. Probably. However, as the story unfolds further and Jacob becomes wealthier than you can possibly imagine, he remembers the vow he made at Bethel. It's easy to promise God access to all of your finances when you are flat broke. The true test comes when you have cash on hand and plenty of money in the bank. Then, what will you do? Will you remember the promise you made? Will you keep your word? Will you stick to the terms of the agreement? Remember, we are building a foundation here so pay attention to the details.

Ok, we are still talking about Jacob at the moment. Why would God really believe that this man who really started out on the wrong foot would actually turn his business around? What would even make God think that Jacob wouldn't relive his past mistakes and cheat again? What was it that made Jacob so different that God took notice of him and blessed him despite his past?

Are you still hindered by your past? Is something in your past still haunting you? You need to settle in your mind once and for all that God looks to what you will become in Him. God knows your past but **He speaks to your future**. It is the enemy who speaks to your past. If he can keep you chained to past failures and mistakes, then he knows that you will never be able to focus on the future. Are you ready to let go of the past and get moving toward your future?

Let's take a moment right here and pause. Some of you reading this book at this very moment are so chained to past failures and mistakes that God is not able to move you into your place of blessing. You are so wrapped up in the bondage of your situation that you cannot see the hand of God reaching out to you in an attempt to lift you from the thoughts that have plagued you for so long. Right now, allow God free access into your heart and soul. Allow Him to wash your mind with the healing power of forgiveness. Take a deep breath and relax. Keep in mind that He is still speaking to your future. Are you ready to proceed on the journey? If so, then let's look together at what made Jacob so different that it began one of the first real examples of true marketplace leadership and blessing.

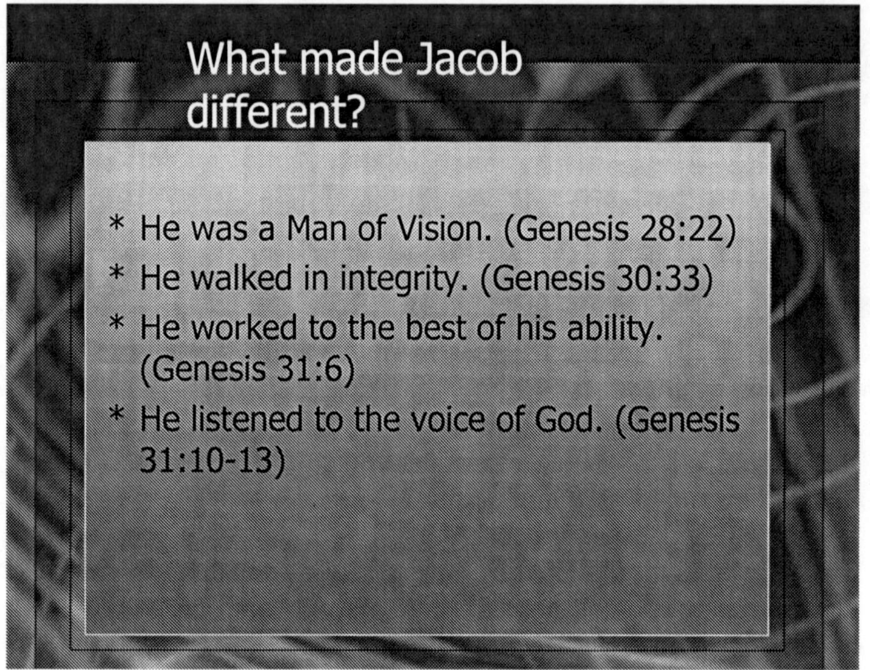

<u>What made Jacob Different?</u>

> **Genesis 28:22 – "And this stone, which I have set up as a pillar (monument), shall be God's house (a sacred place to me): and of all (the increase of possessions) that you give me I will give the tenth to you" (Amplified Version)**

<u>First Difference</u>

He was a man of vision. Think about it. Here he is on the run, knowing that he has been dishonest and to top it off he doesn't have anything to show for it. He got the birthright, but nothing tangible at the moment to hang his future on. In other words, he had no cash. Nada. Nothing. Oh sure the birthright held a promise of wealth, but only if he could ever cash in on it. Since he was on the run, and afraid his brother would find him and kill him, cashing in on this birthright thing was probably not high on his agenda. So, he's back to trying to figure out a way to survive. Sound familiar? Are you just trying to survive and find yourself living paycheck to paycheck?

Now, here' s where the fun begins. Jacob knows he has messed up and realizes that his past will at some point catch up with him. But, for now he is just fine with praying for food to eat and clothes to wear. However, in the midst of what may seem like dire circumstances he still sees a promise for a future. However dim it may be at that moment the fact is that he had a ray of hope that a better day would come. How do we know that? Well, in the midst of his pain, he spoke to his own future. How?

1.) **He built a monument of remembrance**.

He made a place that would be a sacred place for him and God. It would forever signify in his mind, that at that very moment in time he drew a line in the sand and made a promise to God. He knew that God was capable of delivering him. He had seen God's power in the past. As he offered his earnest prayer, he knew that the transforming power of God could change his situation. That moment in time was one of the most significant in his life. Why? During that prayer he laid a foundation of remembrance in his mind as a testament to his faith.

Can you remember the last time you drew a line in the sand and told God that things were going to be different? Have you built any monuments of remembrance of times that you have stood in faith when everything may have seemed hopeless? If you don't have any monuments then why not start now? Stand in faith right now that things are going to change in your career. Stand in faith and believe that your life will bring transformation to those around you. Make this moment a monument of remembrance as you lay the foundation for your future.

2.) **<u>He commits his future wealth to the Lord</u>**

Jacob uses this time as the time to commit his future wealth and increase to the Lord. Remember, at this time he doesn't have a clue as to what is in store for him. So, he's taking a big leap of faith to promise that he will give from his increase. This meant that he had to believe that increase was going to come in the first place. As a man of vision, he knew that despite his past, God wanted to bless him.

If you will choose to commit your business and your future to the Lord, then increase will come. When it comes (and it will) remember your vow. So, as you are laying your foundation remember to commit your increase and your future to the Lord. Then, leave the outcome to Him. He will make sure that increase will follow those who dedicate their business endeavors to His kingdom advancement.

> **Genesis 30:33 – "So later when the matter of my wages is brought before you, my fair dealing will be evident and answer for me..." (Amplified)**

<u>Second Difference</u>

He was a man of integrity. Don't laugh yet. Ok, I know what you are thinking. You are thinking of the stolen birthright. You are thinking about the little deceiver. After all, he is a dirty rotten scoundrel isn't he? The past does tend to follow you doesn't it? Here's what I find amazing. Now that Jacob is well into his little business venture it appears he has learned his lesson. The days of cheating are over. How do we know that? Well, according to verse 33 he is willing for "his fair dealings" to be evidence on his wages. Now that's a bold statement for anyone let alone someone with a less than stellar reputation. If your work habits were to control your wages and speak on your behalf, what would your habits say?

Jacob is so confident that he has cleaned up his act that he is willing to lay his money on the line. Not bad for someone who had such a rough start. Are you getting the picture? You may have started out on the wrong foot but you don't have to remain there. You have the ability to change your circumstances and build the right foundation. You have the choice to allow your work to be a testament to the type of wages you deserve. Again, I humbly ask, if that were true, what pay should you receive? Think about it. Be a person of integrity and your work will speak for itself. Jacob is making progress. Are you?

> **Genesis 31:6 – "You know that I have served your father with all my might and power." (Amplified)**

Third Difference

He worked to the best of his ability. This principle is fairly simple. Give your boss the best work you can possibly give. When you perform a task do you give it all you have? Are you a portrait of excellence or mediocrity? Jacob was able to point to his work ethic and allow it to speak on his behalf. Part of building a strong foundation is the simple principle of providing excellence in every area of your professional career. Remember our earlier lessons? Can you look at your professional life and really say that you do everything with excellence? If so, great! If not, then add that to the list of things needed for a strong foundation.

> **Genesis 31:10-13 – "And I had a dream at the time the flock conceived. I looked up and saw that the rams which mated with the she-goats were streaked, speckled, and spotted. And the Angel of God said to me in the dream, Jacob. And I said, Here am I. And He said, Look up and see, all the rams which mate with the flock are streaked, speckled, and mottled; for I have seen all that Laban does to you. I am the God of Bethel, where you anointed the pillar, and where you vowed a vow to Me. Now arise, get out from this land, and return to your native land." (Amplified)**

Fourth Difference

He listened to the voice of God. This is the most important lesson in the principles of foundation and in understanding the economy of God. There are many nuggets applicable to business in these few verses of scripture. Let's break them down shall we?

1)God speaks to Jacob in a dream. First, let me say that I don't believe that every single dream you have is a message from heaven. However, there are times when God will use a dream to speak a message directly to your spirit. You will know when this happens. In this particular passage we see that God used the dream to speak to Jacob about ram and goat future trading. If you study this part of the story in depth you will find that God instructs Jacob exactly how and when to "mate" his particular flock. In simple terms, God told Jacob how to control his economy. Think about it. If you knew what products or services were going to be the hottest thing going next quarter wouldn't that make a difference in your approach to business? Now, pardon me for just a moment as I speak frankly to make a point. If God knows what goat and ram futures will be the hottest thing to hit the market, then I ask you, don't you think he knows what will make your marketplace flourish and reproduce? Pay attention to the voice of God. He may just be preparing you for the economy ahead. He knows your future. As you dedicate your business endeavors to Him, ask Him to speak into your life the direction you have been seeking. Remember the **Principle of the Open Door**? Use those open doors that He places before you as the springboard to your next idea, product or service. Again, He wants your business to increase so that His kingdom rule can advance and true transformation will occur in your marketplace sphere of influence.

2)God notices how you are treated. I find this most comforting. Notice in the verses above that God speaks to Jacob and tells him that He sees all that Laban has done to him. So, don't think that your boss can mistreat you and get away with it. God sees. He will cause you to flourish despite the treatment of your boss. Your boss does not control your economy. God does. Some of you are so distressed over the way you are being treated on your job. Take heart. God will vindicate you. I have found this to be true many times in my own career. I have had bosses who broke a promise, or gave someone else credit for something I did, or took a trip that I had won, etc. etc. etc. In the end, it really doesn't matter. God knows. He keeps a complete tab on all the wrongs that have been done to us. He will make sure that our economy never suffers if we entrust it to His control. So, rest easy my friend. Your boss can't hide forever. God will make sure that everyone gets what they deserve. We'll chat more about this in our lessons on covenant.

3)God remembers Jacob's vow. Now this should really speak to you. God gives Jacob the answers to the hottest product questions, takes note of his treatment by his boss Laban, and remembers the day that the line in the sand was drawn. God always remembers the promises we make. He reminded Jacob that He remembered as well. Why is this so important? As God remembers our vow, He delivers His instruction for blessing. So, what does He tell Jacob to do? He says, arise and go back to your native land. Translation. Get up buddy and head home. Think about this for a minute. He could have told him to go anywhere but he didn't. He told him to head home. Why? Wasn't home the place that he feared the most? After all, his brother was probably just waiting for him to return so he could kill him. Can you imagine the thoughts that were going through his mind at the time? He longed to see his family but wondered what would happen to him if he did return. There are some instructions that will never make logical sense. But, Jacob needed to be able to free himself from those past mistakes. **<u>There are times that you have to confront your past to accept the blessings of the future.</u>** I don't know what instruction you will be given to go and take your promise. However, of one thing I am sure. You will find the promise as you build the foundation of your career with the core principles that we have just established. God is waiting on you to start down this journey. Once you do, He is responsible for the final destiny.

SEVENTH LESSON: GOD KNOWS MY PAST BUT SPEAKS TO MY FUTURE!

Questions to consider:

1.) Do you currently walk in authority in your marketplace?
2.) Have you kept track of the vows you've made?
3.) Are you a person of vision?
4.) Are you a person of integrity?
5.) Do you work with excellence?
6.) Do you listen to the instruction of God?
7.) Can you identify a monument of remembrance?

Chapter Eight - The Principle of Accountability

The Principle of Accountability is something that will radically affect your marketplace survival and success. Would you consider yourself the lone ranger at the moment? Are you out there in the commerce jungles facing the giants' all alone? Do you make major decisions without proper council? In order for any business to survive it is important to have a close circle of advisors who hold us accountable. Many of them may be our armor bearers as we discussed in the previous chapter. Some of them may be Pastors or teachers that are speaking into our lives. They may also be other marketplace warriors that have joined forces with you. Can you name these individuals right now? Let me help you. These are the guys and gals that you go to for advice, prayers, and support. However, accountability is a deeper level of relationship than most. It is a deep commitment on the part of both of you. You must be willing to open your heart and mind to the council they provide and be willing to be corrected and oftentimes mentored by them.

The Principle of Accountability brings with it a special bond between a group or team of people. It grants those few access into your life at a deeper level than any other. You have given the right to these people to speak the truth (in love) and gently remind you when your life is out of focus or when your business is going down the wrong path. When I ask someone to hold me accountable then I give him or her permission to the deepest part of my soul. It is a relationship that I don't treat lightly. I have people in ministry and within the marketplace that I have asked to be my accountability partners.

Many times they have prayed with me concerning a matter and have rejoiced as we saw the victory together. Other times, they have gently corrected me of wrong behavior or actions and have reminded me of my commitment to the Lord. In these relationships getting offended is never allowed. Why? This team of individuals are the ones that God places around you that love you, pray for you, advise you, comfort you, rejoice with you, cry with you, and generally have your total victory and success as their primary concern. They love you unconditionally. They love you when you're wrong or when you're right. They love you despite any of your flaws. They are your best cheerleaders and deepest confidants.

If you don't have this team around you then pray earnestly that God will direct them to you. They will be the ones holding you as you cross the finish line to victory even if you don't have the strength to get there yourself. Let's take a peek into how God blesses Jacob as he remains accountable to those around him, as well as, to God.

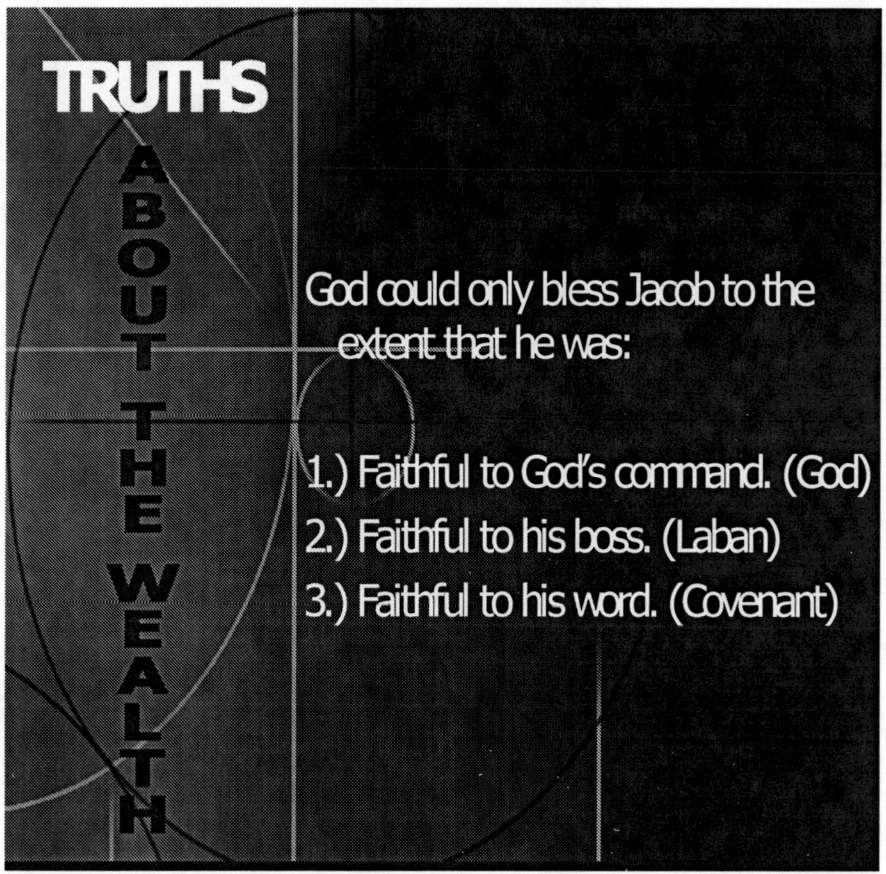

Why was Jacob blessed with Wealth?

Truths about the Wealth

What really brings wealth? Simply put, it is accountability. It is our ability to be held liable or responsible to the commands and behavior that God will require of us. In today's politically correct society this word is almost never used anymore. Our society has gotten used to blaming someone else. You can almost hear the collective chant that we did nothing wrong, it was the other person's fault. But, if we are to establish true marketplace dominion we better learn this lesson early. Do you find yourself looking at others and casting blame in their direction? Are you always looking for a scapegoat upon whom to put pressure? Do you hear yourself speaking as if the entire failure of your company rests squarely on someone else's shoulder?

At some point we must be true to ourselves and to God. In the end the only one that will answer for your marketplace is YOU! If you are really looking to walk into financial dominion in your professional life then you must be faithful to the marketplace, and those in it, before God can bestow upon you the fullness of the blessings He has prepared for you. Again, let's look at Jacob. Jacob's marketplace shows us our "best practice" model for success. God could only bless Jacob to the extent that he was:

1.) Faithful to God's command
2.) Faithful to his boss
3.) Faithful to his word

How did Jacob's life affect his marketplace?

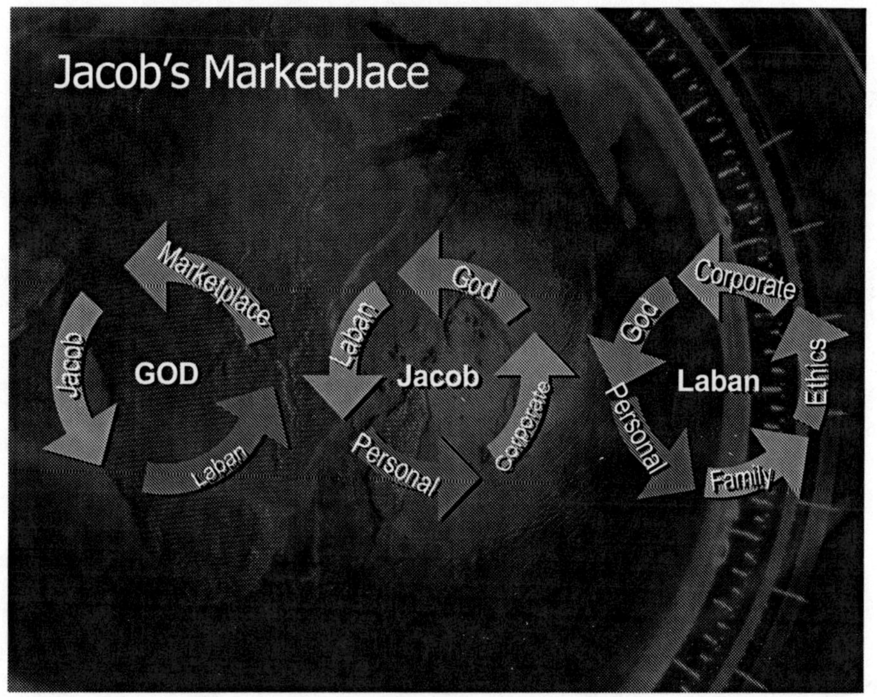

So, let's look at Jacob's marketplace in depth, as we also consider our own. Look at the above diagram closely. Do you see three areas operating within Jacob's economic world? Also notice that within each of these areas are "sub-areas" that will affect that particular part of your life. So as noted above, each of our marketplace endeavors will have three major areas at work. We will have God, our boss, and our own work ethics, values and covenants to consider. Remember, God can only bless us to the extent that we are faithful to our assignments. Hang in there with me on this chapter. It may not be the most fun, but it will produce the greatest results! With that in mind, let's get started shall we?

First Area Of Marketplace Accountability

God can only bless us to the extent that we are faithful to Him. We have discussed at length thus far how much God wants to be a part of our professional career. He delights in your growth process and rejoices every time you include Him in your business decisions. Part of growing and maturing as a Christian is our ability to let go and let God take over. Sometimes growth is a very painful process. Do you remember as a child getting those horrible leg cramps in the middle of the night? Then someone in the family would offer their opinion and say, "oh, they are just growing pains." At the time you probably wanted to slap them. But, by the end of the year, guess what? You could actually measure the growth that took place. You could see tangible results for the pain you encountered. Our growth as Kings and Queens is no different. Each time a growth process takes place we can rest in the realization that a tangible result will soon follow.

Although it may seem an insignificant change at first, you will eventually be able to put a definite measure on the growth that has occurred. Finding your mission in the marketplace is not easy, but it will be rewarding. It will also bring the most fruit as you pursue only those things that are truly worthy of your passion and commitment. How do you get the answer to finding your mission? You must include God in every decision you make. Remember from our earlier discoveries that God has had an eye on you since you were conceived? He knew exactly what talents and skills you were going to possess. He put them there. Why not start including the one who created you in on your business endeavors? Be true to your commitment to Him, and He will take care of everything else.

Since we have decided to include God in our business and professional lives let's chat about what that means. Once we include Him, then our conduct and attitudes for approaching business should be radically different. Isaiah 48:17 says,

> **"Thus, says the Lord, your Redeemer, the Holy One of Israel: I am the Lord your God who teaches you to PROFIT, who leads you by the way that you should go." (Amplified)**

After reading this verse it is hard to imagine that we would ever make any decisions without the input from God. Wow! Did you notice that God promises to **TEACH** us to **PROFIT** and to lead us in the way we should go? If He is the willing teacher then shouldn't we be a willing student? But, more often than not we find ourselves trying to plan, strategize, manipulate or maneuver our way to the top. You may be thinking to yourself, well, I can't believe that God really has time to devote to my needing another idea for business growth. Is He really concerned about my shrinking bottom line? Does ROI really matter to Him? Well, let me help you with the answer if you haven't figured it out already. If He (God) is willing to teach you to PROFIT, what do you think?

The word PROFIT should give us a clue into His intent for us. In fact He does care about the bottom line, ROI and everything else that affects your life in your marketplace dealings. After all, the less profit you make, the less His kingdom can advance. Are you getting the picture now? He wants to help you. He will teach you what to do. He will lead you exactly where you should go. I may not understand every nuance of your particular field, but I know someone who does! He's just waiting on an invitation from you to start the learning process. So, what do you say? Need a little help on increasing your profits? Well, now you know where to go.

Second Area Of Marketplace Accountability

God can only bless us to the extent that we are faithful to our boss. Before you say anything I know what some of you are thinking. You are thinking, "Yeah, but you don't know my boss." Was I right? It still doesn't change the fact that God expects you to submit to your boss and be a faithful employee. That is the only way that we can seek His hand of blessing on our efforts. Now before you can go any further in your commentary about how bad your boss is let's check out Jacob's boss Laban, shall we?

As an employee and a boss myself I find this story to be fascinating. As a boss Laban failed. He was a cheater and deceiver himself. But, I find it interesting that Jacob had to face this particular battle. Remember how he started his business? He used deception to steal his brother's birthright. Well, low and behold what do you think he encountered in some of his first business dealings? Bingo. You guessed it. He encountered deception and down right theft. Although you will be forgiven for any unethical activity, you will still have to pay up at some point in your career. This was Jacob's pay up time if you will. But, notice that even though Jacob had to encounter the same thing that he dealt to his brother, God still blessed him. God would not allow him to be hurt. In Genesis 31:6-7 Jacob says,

> **"You know that I have served your father with all my might and power. But your father has deceived me, and changed my wages ten times; but God did not allow him to hurt me. If he said, The speckled shall be your wages, then all the flock bore speckled; and if he said, The streaked shall be your hire, then all the flock bore streaked."**

Again, notice that Jacob was able to say that even though he was treated wrongly, he walked in integrity. His work ethic is what allowed the blessing to come to him. So no matter what your boss does to you if you can truly say that you are working for him or her with all your power and might, then nothing they can do to you can hurt you.

The life lesson here is that there will probably never be a perfect boss. But, God controls your economy and your destiny, not your boss. As long as you are faithful to give your boss excellence in everything you do then profits are sure to follow. You must be diligent in your efforts. Stop giving a halfhearted effort as you grind through your daily activities. If you want the blessing of the Lord then you must be diligent in planning your success and strategies for growing your business. Proverbs 21:5 says,

"The plans of the diligent lead to profit..."

So stop blaming your boss for your condition. Stop blaming the company because you can't get by. Start giving them 110%, and then watch what God will do. Are you being faithful to your boss now? Do you find yourself talking bad about him behind his back? Do you question her authority at every turn? Do you find yourself resenting the treatment you are getting? Well, turn it over to God. Give it to Him. Then, make your work a testament to God's kingdom. When you are faithful to His commands, then he will make sure that you are blessed. When God is in control of your marketplace the final outcome is up to Him. We will talk about the relationship between a company owner and employee in our section on covenant.

Third Area Of Marketplace Accountability

God can only bless us to the extent that we are faithful to His word. Throughout your journey in the marketplace you will be held accountable to the word of God regarding your business endeavors and your own personal word. As you seek God's guidance for direction for your business be prepared to follow through with the instructions that He gives you. As he gives you an idea be quick to incorporate it into your daily routine. Can you imagine how Jacob must have felt when God gave him the dream about how to direct his flock in their "procreation" process? He could have written that dream off as some very bad pita bread. But, instead he immediately began to change the course of how he tended his flocks. As soon as he did, his flocks began to multiply like crazy and became the strongest in the flock. Remember, God wants to teach you to PROFIT. Had any really far out ideas lately? Maybe you need to run a sanity check. Perhaps those ideas were heaven sent. ☺

Not long ago I was praying about a particular deal that I was working on and asking God for divine direction. As I prayed, I got a detailed plan revealed to me. As I chatted with the Lord about it He gave me a clear word. He said, "**Specific intent requires specific**

instruction." Translation? There are times when God will lay out before you specific instructions that are detailed to the minute level. Those are the ones you need to really pay attention to. When you receive really specific instructions then you can bet that there is a specific intent for your life at that moment. Don't take any shortcuts in this situation. Do everything exactly the way He commands. That is when the true blessing and profit will come. I encourage you to read Genesis chapters 29-32 and see how Jacob prospered from following specific instructions.

In addition to being faithful to the Word of God we must also watch over our own word. Our commitments and promises in the marketplace will make a statement about the true nature of our relationship with God. He expects us to keep our word. He expects us to be people of integrity. Do you ever make flippant statements knowing full well that you never intend to do whatever it is you just promised?

Do you recall our discussion about the power of your word when we first got started? As we are building our Kingdoms it is important to recognize that our word is one of the most important things about how we conduct our business affairs. When you give your word to a client do they need to see it in 30 different "written" formats just to be assured that they will be covered? There will be times when keeping your word will cost you. These will be times of testing for you and your company. However, it will be what separates your business as something different.

As part of my particular job function I have to respond to very lengthy Requests for Proposals (RFP). In my response it is my responsibility to adequately follow the parameters of the RFP while also bidding in such a way that our company makes a profit. On one such occasion, I was working on a proposal along with one of our lead Project Managers. We had worked on our response for almost a month. Somewhere in the many iterations and variations of our response we made a very small error. We left off one letter of a part number that was to be used in this project. No one in the company caught this little snafu. To make a very long story short, it was after we got awarded the project and were half way into the job that we discovered the difference that one little letter made. It would cost our company money to make it right. We could have probably skipped by and no one would have been the wiser. However, part of our company mission statement is that we work with integrity. Now, this is when the true test of character takes place. I had to go in and tell our boss that this one little letter would cost us a few thousand dollars and thus lessen our profit margin on the job. I reminded him of our commitment to excellence and told him that in the long run everything would be okay. So, we went to the customer and told them of our mistake. I wish I could tell you they were so impressed that we were honest that they offered to pay us anyway. But, they didn't. However, we are still doing business with that customer today because we chose to take the path of truth. Keeping your word isn't always easy. Keeping your word isn't always convenient. It is however a necessity if you arc seeking blessing for your marketplace.

Your word holds power far beyond anything you can imagine. It is what makes the intangible, tangible. Your word is what brings things from the spiritual realm into the physical realm. As powerful as it is it can also be our undoing. How many promises and commitments have you made and then didn't follow through? Have you told a customer, "I'll have that for you tomorrow" and then let a week or two go by with no results? Let your word speak volumes about who and what you stand for. It will be the avenue for blessing for your efforts in the future.

As we bring this chapter to a close it is important to realize how much Jacob was blessed by following **The Principle of Accountability**. Jacob was blessed both professionally and personally as he put these principles into practice. Genesis 30:43 says,

> **"Thus the man became exceedingly prosperous and had large flocks, female and male servants, and camels and donkeys."**

Notice that he acquired additional items along the way. The original arrangement included sheep, goats and lambs. But when he left for home he also had servants, camels, donkeys, and a large family. God wants to bring increase to EVERY area of your life. God gave him supernatural wisdom and ability to increase in all areas of his life.

Here's an added bonus. Laban was blessed because of Jacob. Laban knew that God was including him on Jacob's blessing. Genesis 20:27 says,

> **"And Laban said to him, "Please stay, if I have found favor in your eyes, for I have learned by experience that the Lord has blessed me for your sake."**

So what does this mean for you? It means that if you are an employee God will bless the business because of you. If you are an owner of a company and you employ true marketplace leaders, then your business will increase simply because of their faithfulness. How cool is that? Either way, your business will be blessed. Can you imagine the power of a company that has multiple marketplace leaders dedicating the business to God? Wow! That company would truly be unstoppable. Bosses, pay attention to any employee that you retain that also offers prayers on your behalf. It may be the very thing that will help you to prosper and profit in spite of the economy. So, go out there in faith and with accountability and see what God will do for you. He's waiting to bless you.

EIGHTH LESSON: I MUST SURROUND MYSELF WITH A TEAM OF INDIVIDUALS WHO WILL HOLD ME ACCOUNTABLE FOR MY ACTIONS.

Questions to consider:

1.) Do you have a team of accountability partners currently?
2.) Do you allow them free access into every area of your life?
3.) Do you readily make adjustments to your character to fully

ensure that Christ will be honored?

4.) Are you willing to remain accountable even if it costs you something?

Chapter Nine - The Principle of Covenant

What is a Covenant and why is it Important?

The Principle of Covenant is one of the most important lessons that you will learn on the journey. (Business Owners Pay Special Attention) The ability to abide by and fulfill a covenant will be the single most important test to determine whether or not you are truly committed to a marketplace that is centered around and dedicated to the Lord. So what is covenant, and why is it so important?

According to Webster's dictionary, a covenant is a formal contract or a binding agreement. It could also be considered a solemn pledge. As you approach your marketplace it is vital that you understand how many times you enter into covenants within a typical day. As you enter into these agreements please understand that God places special importance on them. Again, this should jog our memory on how much our word means to the life of our business. So, let's look at just a few types of covenants as they may relate to our workplace. I have listed a few examples below, and then we'll take a look at some examples of covenant within the Bible.

- An employment contract with an employee

- A contract with a customer
- A contract with a vendor
- A partnership arrangement with another company

Did you ever wonder when the first covenant (pledge, promise) was first mentioned in the Bible? It was just prior to the great flood. According to the Bible, Noah was a just man. He was a man of impeccable character and integrity. In fact in Genesis 6:9 we read, **"…Noah was a just man, perfect in his generations. Noah walked with God."** The circumstances of Noah's day were quite dim. Around him were violence, chaos and destruction. You might say that his marketplace had gone to the animals. (Don't laugh I was tempted to say it went to the dogs)

The world was so corrupt that God decided to destroy it and start all over. But, prior to this catastrophic event, God lays out a detailed plan for the ark and for the preservation of a remnant of people and livestock. The encouraging lesson here is that even if your marketplace is flooding in around you, as long as you walk in integrity with God, He will sustain you and provide you with a means of escape. The power of the covenant God made with Noah is still evident today. Each time we look to the sky and see a rainbow we are reminded of a promise made and a promise kept.

Are the covenants we make as long lasting? Can they or will they affect future generations? Would it surprise you to know that whatever place you may find yourself in at the moment can be profoundly affected by a covenant?

Remember when we started on this journey together a few pages ago? At that time we dedicated our work, our professional lives, and everything within us to the power of God. At that time we entered into a covenant with the great Creator. From that time forward all of our decisions should be based on the relationship that we have with Him. You may be thinking that you have made too many mistakes for God to care about the things you are experiencing. You may be thinking that there is no way that a Holy God could live around the mess you have made of your business endeavors. No doubt some of you are still haunted by past mistakes and perhaps some unscrupulous business deals. Can God take what you have and redeem it? The answer is a whole hearted YES! Jeremiah 31:33-34 should give you comfort. Read the promise of God below,

> **"But this is the covenant that I will make with the house of Israel after those days, says the Lord: I will put my law in their minds, and write it on their hearts, and I will be their God, and they shall be my people. No more shall every man teach his neighbor, and every man his brother, saying, "Know the Lord, for they all shall know me, from the least of them to the greatest of them, says the Lord. For I will forgive their iniquity, and their sin I will remember no more."**

You need to establish in your mind once and for all that God stands ready and waiting to forgive any mistakes that you may have made in the past. **He is fully capable of dealing with your past while at the same time speaking to your future**. If you turn your marketplace over to Him, then trust him to give you the necessary advice and counsel that will guard all of your possessions and potential. The future still holds the promise of greatness for you. God knows in order for you to walk into the destiny that your covenant with Him prepares, you must have a marketplace that produces for you. Notice that for all of those who gave the control over to God, there was supernatural protection from the calamities that were to come.

Are you consumed with fear about the economy and how it will affect you? Do you dwell on how you will be able to make it next year, or the following year? If God is truly in control, then do your best and leave the final results to Him. It will sure help maintain a healthy blood pressure for you! If you take the time to study those who were in covenant with God you will see one common thread in each of their lives. He always warned them if something was going to be a threat to them, and He also provided them a way of escape. So, stop loosing sleep over things that haven't even happened yet. Let go of the control button, and give it to God. He can take care of all that concerns you.

Well, by now I'm sure you get the picture. God wants to protect you and yours so that His kingdom can be advanced. Jacob is a prime example of the power of a covenant with God. Remember, Jacob's economic plan was not affected by changes in pay or in the terms of his employment. He knew that his benefits package with God included the protection of all that was his despite anything that his boss tried to do. So, let's check back in on Jacob. First, remember that Jacob started his business at Bethel with a covenant (binding agreement, contract) with God. As he concludes his conversation and negotiation with God he heads over to his Uncle Laban's house to his first job interview. Pay attention to this part of the story if you are seeking a job. There is a huge lesson here. Genesis 29:15 in the Amplified version says,

> **"Then Laban said to Jacob, just because you are my relative, should you work for me for nothing? Tell me, what shall your wages be?"**

One of the most important lessons you can learn as you approach the job market is to know your value prior to negotiating any contract. As the scripture above reveals it was the first thing on the agenda as Laban was preparing a work relationship. You must be ready to answer this question. What are you worth? When you step into a company seeking employment or if you are in the office of your boss hoping to obtain a raise can you answer that one simple question? What do you want your wages to be? You'd be surprised how many people truly cannot answer this question. If you can't answer it, then you probably won't get what you are expecting. Your boss is not a mind reader. Be ready to tell him or her what you expect. There is one thing I can guarantee. You will NEVER get what you don't ask for. Now, let's study the second part of the arrangement for Jacob's employment.

Laban makes a covenant with Jacob and agrees to give his daughter Rachel to Jacob if he works for seven years. (This was probably the first employment agreement recorded) As a business owner you make covenants or contracts with employees every time you hire someone to fill a position. Whether or not it is actually written out is not the point. If you hire someone and promise them a salary, bonuses, car allowance etc., then as a Christian employer you might want to study this story in depth. It will give you a clear understanding as to what happens to a boss who doesn't hold up his end of the bargain.

Jacob worked for Laban for seven years and kept his covenant. He did exactly what he said he was going to do as part of their contract. But, at the end of his seven years of toil instead of waking up after the wedding night with his beloved Rachel he finds himself married to Leah. His boss and father in law had deceived him. So, the deceiver had been deceived. It is true that your sins will follow you. Even though your sins have been forgiven, the seed that was sown will still have a harvest. (Remember, even a seed sown by mistake will produce.) So, the first employment agreement was officially broken. Now, let's stop right here for a moment. Are you a boss? Have you made promises to employees that you have not kept? Have you reneged on a deal to an employee, vendor or customer? God will hold you accountable for your actions. Just as Jacob had to pay for his deception with his brother, his boss Laban, will pay as well. There is an old but true saying. "What goes around comes around." It is another way of saying that you will indeed reap what you sow.

Now, Jacob is faced with a dilemma, should he trust a boss that has cheated him once already? Will he be cheated again? Well, it doesn't take him long to consider his options. As he ponders life without Rachel, whom he loves beyond description, he knows he has no choice but to accept the new arrangement that Laban offers. Jacob must work another seven years to be allowed to have Rachel. All, I can say is that she must have been some kind of woman to get a man so devoted to her that he would work for 14 years for a boss that cheated him on multiple occasions and changed his "wages" ten times. Sound familiar? How many of you have worked for a company that continually changes the rules of engagement in their favor despite any previous pledges, promises or commitments? Would you have given as much dedication as Jacob? Would you have still performed your job with excellence despite how you were being treated? Jacob did.

We've considered Jacob's part of the story but what about Laban? Remember in this particular relationship that Laban was the master of his house and was the one who had the power to make the decisions for the family and for his business. However, after Jacob began building his own flock (kingdom, business empire) we read in Genesis 30:27-28 how the tables have turned. No longer is Jacob asking for a job. Rather, Laban is pleading saying,

> **"And Laban said to him, If I have found favor in your sight, I pray you (do not go); for I have learned by experience and from the omens in divination that the lord has favored me with blessings on your account.**
> **He said, state your salary, and I will give it."**

Wow, can you imagine the humbling that Laban took when he had to do that? He is forced to practically beg one of his employees to stay with him. He realizes that without Jacob, his business will not prosper to the extent that it will under Jacob's authority. At least this CEO was keenly aware who holds all the cards in this arrangement. Laban knows that Jacob is the key to the success of his business and his household.

May I gently remind all of you who consider yourself to be the boss or who may own the business that it is much easier to treat an employee with integrity and fairness from the start than to cheat them and then have to beg them to come back. If you ever find yourself in the position that you have to get an employee back you will find as Laban did that the price is much higher than if you would have kept your promises in the first place. Let's consider the next business transaction that unfolds as we read in Genesis 30: 29-34. This exchange happens right after Laban asks him to name his salary.

> **"Jacob answered him, You know how I have served you, and how your possessions, your cattle and sheep and goats, have fared with me. For you had little before I came, and it has increased and multiplied abundantly; and the Lord has favored you with blessings wherever I turned. But now when shall I provide for my own house also? Laban said, What shall I give you? And Jacob said, You shall not give me anything. If you will do this one thing for me and I will again feed and take care of your flock. Let me pass through all of your flock today, removing from it every speckled and spotted animal and every black one among the sheep, and the spotted and speckled among the goats; and such shall be my wages. So later when the matter of my wages is brought before you, my fair dealing will be evident an answer for me. Everyone that is not speckled and spotted among the goats and black among the sheep , if found with me, shall be counted as stolen. And Laban said, "Well: let it be done as you say."**

To make a very long story short, even though Laban agreed to the terms of the new employment contract he didn't even let the ink dry before he started modifying the arrangement. Verse 35 of Genesis chapter 30 tells us that the same day the agreement was forged; Laban went and had all of the flocks that should have been Jacob's transferred to the care of his sons. Either he was extremely stupid or had a death wish. He knew that his business would not be the same without Jacob. He knew that Jacob was the reason his business was growing larger and stronger by the day. But, he cheated Jacob once again and stole his part of the agreement. Remember, whatever seed you sow will produce a harvest. Keep that in mind as we continue in our study.

If you continue reading the story you will find that God gave Jacob an ingenious idea on how to increase his flock. As he followed this new strategy he found that his flock grew stronger and larger than

Laban's flock. Not only did his flock (business) grow but so did every other part of Jacob's life. He was becoming a man of great wealth. God promises to give you the inventions necessary to make you a success in your particular field. You do not have to worry about where the inspiration will come from if you are totally dedicated to Him.

Remember, it is His responsibility to take care of you. Has your business grown stagnated? Do you find yourself just going through the motions of the day? Has the working world left you an empty shell? Have you been in overdrive trying to make everything happen all by yourself? If you answered yes to any of these questions you need to remind yourself about ***The Principle of Covenant***. It is God's sovereign word to complete and protect everything that concerns you. He doesn't enter into these contracts lightly and neither should you. He promises to bring you through things that may even seem like the deepest valley you have every faced. You may not always be delivered from the valley, but you will never be alone there.

If you are a business owner then you need to read the story of Jacob and Laban with a new understanding. You need to realize that God is very attentive to how you treat your employees and the covenants that you make with Him and them. If you promise something to your staff, then do it. If you have a contract with a vendor or customer then abide by the contract. When you promise a customer that you will deliver a product without damage by a certain time then make sure your word is kept. If your package arrives late then don't assume that everything is still ok between you and the customer. Let them know that your word is very important to you by showing your concern over the late arrival. If you are in partnership with another company then protect that alliance as if the fate of your business depended on it. (and it may)

These are just a few practical examples of types of covenants that are represented in the marketplace today. Suffice it to say that God is a keeper of His word, and He expects you to do the same. The purpose of God is that you keep every single word that you utter from your mouth. A simple word to the wise employer would be this. Don't try to cheat an employee. (Especially not a Christian one) God will always make sure that they come out with the best in all transactions. They may have to suffer loss for a season, but their latter will be greater than how they began. Wouldn't you much rather that your business be blessed because of the life of a believer in the ranks of your staff? In fact, it may be that their presence there is what brings the blessing. So, never underestimate the covering that God places over someone who dedicates his or her professional life to the Lord. He will watch over that business and that person to ensure success.

The first part of this section has concentrated on the covenants that we make with God and within our sphere of business. Now, let's consider the Covenant that God makes with all of us who call ourselves a King. It is important to know that God wants to establish His word to us as we approach our kingdom purposes. So, once again let's look at the scripture to find our reference point. Let's consider 2nd Samuel the 7th chapter for this part of our study.

When kings place their life in the control of the Heavenly Father, then He seeks to enter into a covenant relationship with them. It is exciting when you compare the covenant that God made with David to the covenant that He wishes to make with you. The first verse of that chapter says,

> **"Now it came to pass when the king was dwelling in his house..."**

Notice in this scripture that David was exactly where he was supposed to be at that time. He was in his house. God is looking for a King who will stay in the place of anointing to which He has gifted them. How often do we get excited or move in tangents instead of walking in the gifting and talents that we know we have. Where is your passion? Where do you have the most success? Perhaps, that is the very place that God has destined for you to make the most impact for His kingdom. How often have you watched successful individuals fall flat on their face as they try to move into a new area while others seem to make transitions with ease? From now on, before you make any critical move in career or consider a major life change, ask God if that is the direction that you should move toward. If you don't get a release then, **STAY PUT! Sometimes the greatest blessing is just staying right where you are and being faithful.**

The second part of the first verse gives us all hope. It says that God had given David rest from all of his enemies. Isn't that something to look forward to? There will be those moments in our career where everything is moving in perfect balance and you and the business seem unstoppable. These are the moments to cherish. It is a moment of rest that God has provided for you. Take advantage of these moments. Proverbs 16:7 says,

> **"When a man's ways are pleasing to the Lord…even his enemies live at peace with him."**

In verse two you will notice David making an audible declaration as to where God was dwelling. He was cognizant of where the presence of God dwelt. How often do you make a mental note or check the status of God's presence in your life? If you notice that His presence is not where you want it to be, do you take corrective action to repair any holes in your spiritual armor? Do you take steps to realign your activity so that you invite His presence? To continue toward the goal of kingdom advancement you must always be aware of where God is at every moment. It is critical that He remain the central theme of your professional life.

In verse three of chapter seven we see that the prophet Nathan encourages David to do all that is in his heart. He also reminds him that God will be with him. When a King follows the vision and passion that has been placed in his heart by God, then God is with Him. God wants to direct you in all of your business affairs. As long as you stay within your vision, He will be right there with you to direct your every step. What a comfort to know that God will dwell with us and work within our lives as long as we keep Him as our focus.

> **2 Samuel 7: 8-9 says, "Now therefore, thus shall you say to my servant David, "Thus says the Lord of hosts; I took you from the sheepfold, from following the sheep, to be ruler over my people over Israel.**

And I have been with you wherever you have gone, and have cut off all your enemies from before you, and have made you a great name, like the name of the great men who are on the earth.""

What does this scripture tell you? God remembers where you came from and still wants to use you for HIS glory? He knows where you started. He knows every part of your life, and He loves you exactly the way you are. You don't need to apologize to God for where you have been. He already knows. He uses those events in your life to shape you into the individual that will be the most effective for His kingdom. Some of you are still trying to hold on to the glory days of the past. You waste countless hours reminiscing about people and/or days that have long past. You spend time trying to rekindle old relationships hoping to bring back the golden years. But, get a truth settled in your spirit right now. If someone can walk out of your life easily then let him or her go. **Your destiny is not dependant upon anyone that has left you.**

There are times when you must pull yourself out of the pit of depression and realize that the thing for which you are mourning is long gone. It is dead. Stop trying to resurrect what God has declared dead. Pick yourself up and look at a bright future. It wasn't until David acknowledged that his baby was dead, that Solomon could be conceived. God has the ability to bring life in the midst of death. Stop holding on to the old ideas thinking they will still work. Stop spending time lamenting the partnership that never was or that ended on a sour note. Realize that God now stands ready to take you at this very moment and expand HIS kingdom. Are you ready?

God also knows your present. He knows exactly what you are going through at this very moment. He sees the struggles and the victories. God is in control of your present circumstances as long as you allow Him to have full access to your heart. Be encouraged. Turn every decision over to Him, and He will make the most of your present situation.

In verse 10 of the same chapter we read, "Moreover

> **I will appoint a place for My people Israel, and will plant them, that they may dwell in a place of their own and move no more; nor shall the sons of wickedness oppress them anymore, as previously."**

God knows your future. He has a place prepared for His people. The place that He is preparing for you is a place you can call home. It is a place that is free from oppression. He wants to give you a place where you can rest. The future He prepares for you is one of hope. Start seeing your future the way He sees it. It should encourage you to continue working with your future in mind.

Verse 12 of the same chapter says, **"When your days are fulfilled and you rest with your fathers, I will set up your seed after you, who will come from your body, and I will establish his kingdom. He shall build a house for My name, and I will establish the throne of his kingdom FOREVER.**

Wow, what an incredible verse! God not only has a plan for you, but He has one for your future generations as well. It says that He will set up your seed after you. God has plans for your kingdom to last beyond your lifetime. Do you see why it is so important to make sure your kingdom is on a solid foundation? The principles that you are learning are important for you and those who follow in your footsteps. What an awesome honor and responsibility.

God has a plan to establish your kingdom forever. When you turn your life and your business over to Him then He can build something that will have a legacy for your children and future generations to follow. God wants to be a part of your entire family line so He can bless all of those who will surely follow.

For those of you who may not have children then this could apply to the children that you have "raised" in the Lord or to those you have chosen to mentor. Every leader needs someone that they are mentoring so the baton of the vision can one day be handed to another. It is said that the average person influences at least 10,000 people in their lifetime. Talk about building a kingdom.

Whenever you are in covenant with God, then remember that He cares about your kingdom. He understands your past, is with you in the present, and has great plans for your future. What a comfort to know you are in such good hands.

<u>NINTH LESSON</u>: I MUST HONOR THE COMMITMENTS (COVENANTS) I MAKE TO ENSURE GOD'S BLESSING ON MY LIFE AND MY BUSINESS.

<u>Questions to consider:</u>

1.) Do you enter into commitments without considering the consequences?
2.) Do you pray about the covenants you make before you make them?
3.) Are you aware of any covenants that you are in currently?
4.) Have you broken a covenant and need to ask forgiveness?
5.) Do you fully understand this principle and the importance it has on the growth of your marketplace?

Chapter Ten - The Principle of Favor

What is a Favor and why is it Important?

Have you ever wondered why it seems that certain people get all the breaks? They make everything look so easy. They seem to glide through life without a care in the world. Why do you think that is? Are they better than you? Do they work harder than you? Perhaps the real reason is simple. They may have found the secret called ***The Principle of Favor.*** As a Christian you should know this principle better than anyone. So, let's examine the meaning of favor and see how important it is for the building of a kingdom.

I'm sure you've heard this word bantered around many times. But, is there really a difference for those who have found the secret? If I were to ask you to define favor, could you? Yet, if we are to make a significant impact in those around us we surely need it to survive. Our business needs favor to keep our current customers happy while still attracting new endeavors. Let's face it. We all know we need it. But, what is it really?

According to Webster's dictionary it means preferential treatment, to approve, to assist or to perform a generous act. Did you know that's where the word favorite came from? Have you ever known, I mean really known that you were someone's favorite? Isn't that what we all crave? But, how does that happen? In the world of your marketplace it is critical that you learn this secret early on and you will save yourself a lot of heartache. There have been many occasions when I bow my head at my desk and ask God for favor over a certain contract or a particular customer. Why? Well, I know that when God steps in and gives me favor the heart of the decision maker will literally change right before my eyes. Is that possible? It sure is! Let's take a look at the life of someone who walked in favor with a King and with God.

Have you ever studied the life of Nehemiah? It is a fascinating story of the power that focus can bring. But, it is also a great example of supernatural favor. Let's set the stage for the story and then we'll take a peek at a few scriptures and see how favor changed the course of a man and a nation!

First, I encourage you to read the story for yourself in its entirety. But, for the purposes of our discussion on favor we will move ahead quickly. Ok, since some of you will respond better to the bullet version of the story here goes.

- Nehemiah goes to God in prayer and reminds Him that He is a God who keeps his covenants (word, contract) with those He loves and who have been faithful to Him. (Lesson One…remind God of any covenants the two of you have made)
- Then he asks for forgiveness for all the sins that Israel has committed. (Lesson two…admit that you have made mistakes and ask for forgiveness)
- Then he reminds God of those who have remained faithful (lesson three…it helps if someone in the group has walked in integrity)
- Then according to Nehemiah 1:11 it says,

> "...**Give your servant success today by granting him FAVOR in the presence of this man."**

Ok, you with me so far? Now, let's not forget that Nehemiah has a job. Yep a J.O.B. Sound familiar? Well, he shows up for work at the palace one day and reports to his boss. His boss just happens to be the King. Nehemiah is the cupbearer to the King. I'm not sure what the qualifications were to get this particular assignment but you can bet that it looks good on a resume! The King notices that Nehemiah is sad about something. I find this fascinating in and of itself. It tells me two things. First, Nehemiah must have been a fairly stable, happy go lucky sort of guy. His normal demeanor must have been rather pleasant. Second, the King was a very attentive boss. Let's stop and ponder just one moment on that thought before we go any further. Are you a boss? How often do you recognize when one of your employees seems troubled about something? Are you so preoccupied with your own agenda that you miss the little clues that may be staring you in the face? Let's take a lesson from this boss and be sensitive to the things that are bothering those who serve so faithfully with us.

As the story progresses you will read that the King grants Nehemiah permission to go and rebuild the wall for Israel. Wow! Was it that Nehemiah was some great negotiator? In his own words he says in chapter 2:8,

> **"And because the gracious hand of** my God was upon me, **the king granted my requests."**

So, there are times when the only way you will ever get your request granted is if God places his hand upon you and grants you favor with those with whom you are negotiating. Save yourself a lot of heartache and sleepless nights and just ask for God's help in the first place. Trust me, I've tried it on my own and it is never the same.

Nehemiah begins work on his project and then hits the same wall that you and I face in the working jungle. It's called opposition. I know you know what I'm talking about. See, some of you think just because you were granted favor for access that it is some kind of magic wand that means that the road ahead is smooth sailing. Nothing could be further from the truth. Remember our chat about the armor? Well, you still have it on right? Here's a clue. You keep it on for a reason. That reason is the opposition that you will face along your way. It may be the lies of your competitor. It could be someone within your own organization. But, stay focused! Keep your eye on the finish line. We pick up the story in Chapter 5:15,

> **"But, the earlier governors, those preceding me, placed a heavy burden on the people and took forty shekels of silver from them in addition to food and wine. Their assistants also lorded it over the people. But out of reverence for God I did not act like that. Instead, I devoted myself to the work on this wall."**

This scripture is full of great truths for the marketplace. I love this passage for the message it conveys for those of us in authority. So, here's Nehemiah, the new boss in town. The people (employees) were used to the way the old boss ran things. The old guy loaded them down with work, while decreasing their pay, and then took food right out of their mouth. Ok, it doesn't say it exactly like that but you get the picture. Let's look at it in terms you can understand. The old boss made the employees pick up the slack for anyone that quit or was fired without increasing their pay accordingly. So, that one poor employee down in shipping is now doing four peoples' jobs for the same pay he was getting before. Sound familiar? Ok, if you are the owner of the company I hope you get this message loud and clear. Now, to make matters worse the assistant to the boss has to rub it in. Ok, I can see that you all have the visual for this little setup right now. How do I know? Well, we've all been there before haven't we? Here's the part I love the most. Enter the new boss Nehemiah. The staff (people) is wondering if it's going to be more of the same. But, the new guy surprises them. He's not like the others. What makes him different? It's his reverence for God. It seems that his relationship with God does make a difference. That relationship is what dictated that Nehemiah's behavior could not resemble that of the old boss. He had to be different. He had to treat the employees with respect and keep his head down and do his job. Make sense so far?

Do you really desire change in your job? Then, stop acting like everyone else. Be different. Show the employees what a true relationship with Jesus Christ really means. That is when you will begin to see the change. If you keep reading you will find that Nehemiah explains why he can't act the way the other guys did. He saw the damage that it did to the morale of the people. Are you allowing some of your employees to get away with things they shouldn't? Are there rules for one department that don't apply to another? Why? Does it matter? YES! Nehemiah 5:19 says,

> **"Remember me with favor, O my God, for all I have done for these people."**

At the end of the day why does it matter? The answer is clear. If you want God to grant you favor in your work then he requires that you treat employees (people) with the respect and dignity that you would want. If He were to remember your deeds at this very moment would He be able to grant you favor based on them? That should make you stop and think.

TENTH LESSON: IF I DESIRE TO WALK IN DIVINE FAVOR THEN I MUST LIVE A LIFE OF INTEGRITY.

Questions to consider:

1.) Do you ask for the favor of God to go before you in your marketplace arena?
2.) Can you honestly tell God that you deserve favor based on your treatment of those within your sphere of influence?
3.) What do you do when opposition comes?
4.) Do you walk in the reverence of God and respect those He has placed within your care?
5.) Do you feel you have the right to ask God to remember you with favor based on your actions at work? Nehemiah did.

Chapter Eleven- The Principle of Proper Placement

Do you have the right people in the right place?

The Principle of Proper Placement is one of the most important battle strategies you will learn in our study together. It is critical that you operate within your own particular gifting and strength just as much as your staff. One of the most disturbing tragedies in companies across the globe is to have dedicated employees that are underperforming simply because they are not in the right job category that will best fit their particular skill set. I have seen this within the ranks of companies in which I have worked. Management struggles to understand why one of their "superstars" just can't seem to function in any other department or with any other assignments. It is a given that this employee has been a boost to moral in the past. But, now that they have taken on a new company role the superstar is fading by the moment. What went wrong? Perhaps nothing. It may be that the assignment didn't keep them in the proper placement position best utilizing their skill.

To place an individual by their gifts and talents will ensure that you will get peak performance from them at all times. How do you know what that sweet spot is? It is the individual area or department where they can best shine. It is also where they will be the happiest. For example, not everyone can handle the rejection of sales. Others are driven to madness by the detail that it requires to balance the books. You, or your management staff, must get down in the trenches with them for a while so that you will know where they best fit. Every single person within your company (and life) has a specific place and function where they will shine. It is called ***The Principle of Proper Placement.*** The scripture describes it this way in 1 Corinthians 1:12, 14-27

> **"For just as the body is a unity and yet has many parts, and all the parts, though many, form (only) one body, so it is with Christ, the Messiah, the Anointed One. For the body does not consist of one limb or organ but of many. If the foot should say, because I am not the hand, I do not belong to the body, would it be there not a part of the body? If the ear should say, because I am not the eye, I do not belong the body, would it be therefore not a part of the body? If the whole body were an eye, where would be the sense of hearing? If the whole body were an ear, where would be the sense of smell? But as it is, God has placed and arranged the limbs and organs in the body, each (particular one) of them, just as He wished and saw fit and with the best adaptation. But, if the whole were all a single organ, where would the body be? And now there are certainly many limbs and organs, but a single body. And the eye is not able to say to the hand, I have no need of you, nor again the head to the feet, I have no need of you. But instead, there is absolute necessity for the parts of the**

> **body that are considered the more weak. And those parts of the body which we consider rather ignoble are the very parts which we invest with additional honor; and our unseemly parts and those unsuitable for exposure are treated with seemliness (modesty and decorum), Which our more presentable parts do not require. But God has so adjusted (mingles, harmonized and subtly proportioned the parts of the whole) body, giving the greater honor and richer endowment to the inferior parts which lack apparent importance. So that there is no division or discord or lack of adaptation (of the parts of the body to each other), but the members all alike have a mutual interest in and care for one another. And if one member suffers, all the parts share the suffering; if one member is honored, all the members share in the enjoyment of it. Now you collectively are Christ's body and individually you are members of it, each part severally and distinct, each with his own place and function." (Amplified)**

In order for the marketplace to which you have been assigned to be fully working to its full potential then it is vital that that you understand ***The Principle of Proper Placement*** and the hierarchy that God blesses. It is quite simply this:

<u>God</u>

God has a plan to provide the vision and the anointing for the king in every area of his life. He will help you get to know your employees and their strengths and weaknesses so that you may place them in the best spot for victory. He will guide you to the ones who are ready for battle. He will give you the plans to succeed if you just ask for His assistance. Is every battle easy? No way. But, with the right team around you the victory comes a lot quicker.

King

The king will be blessed by God and given strategies to put in place as he fights the battle for his workplace. As a king seeks the Lord for guidance, then the daily activities of his business will adopt an entirely different mindset. A king must pray for the mind of Christ to be evident in his life. When the mind of Christ rules, then all wisdom and discernment will follow. If you are the owner or manager of the business then you are in a place of authority and as such need the direction of the Lord more than anyone. A lot of tears and worry can be avoided if you simply formulate a team that is grounded in their gifts. It is no longer an option just to fill a spot with a warm body. That never does either party any good. Start praying for the right person to fill each position. Both of you will be much happier.

Kingdom

A king must be willing to fight for his kingdom and to lead it with integrity. God's anointing for blessing will rest upon the man or woman who turns the operation of the business over to Him. God gives the king the power and anointing to rule in his marketplace endeavors. We have been talking about these principles in the previous chapters. Perhaps this will help as you try to remember the responsibilities of the king.

K-A king knows his kingdom.
I-A king intercepts the enemy.
N-A king needs his armor bearer
G-A king gives God full control

How well do you know your staff? Are you still in touch with the heartbeat of the industry? Periodically it is necessary to test your knowledge of the environment that your employees are exposed to on a daily basis. It is easy to become out of touch with those in the ranks if you are not careful. This will only lead to confusion. Your troops are looking for someone they can respect to lead them in the charge against the competition. In order to do that effectively you must realize your own place within the structure of your professional realm.

It is important to remember that a King is fully aware of his anointing by God. **1 Samuel 10:1 says "…Is it not because the Lord has anointed you commander over His inheritance?"** God will give you the abilities to lead and protect the inheritance or business that He has placed within your power and grasp. You may be looking around right now and thinking that he picked the wrong person. Perhaps you were placed in a position of authority by attrition. At this point it really doesn't matter how you got there. What does matter is the principles you allow to guide your decision making process. By using ***The Principle of Proper Placement*** you can guarantee a work environment that is functional and fun at the same time. This principle is vital to success.

A king also knows the vision of his kingdom. (We will talk about that in more detail in the next chapter) Each of you has within you a particular level of talent that God has placed within you. He placed those skills and visions within you because He has chosen you to fulfill a destiny that was specifically designed for you. (Just think….it was Lydia's business of selling purple fabric that helped finance Paul's ministry to the continent of Asia. She was vital to the success of that ministry and to the spread of Christianity in Europe. Her focus and vision in the business arena allowed Paul to walk in his destiny and fulfill his calling to Asia.)

In the life cycle of every business there will come a time when the business owner (king) will be looked upon to provide the winning battle strategy. All businesses will at some point have to go to war! It may be to eek out a higher gross profit to keep the investors happy. It could be to push ahead in new market verticals that will expand your current territory. Whatever the reason, there is a constant battle against those in the workplace. You must pray and ask God to provide you with discernment against all the assignments of the enemy against your business and personal life. Don't kid yourself into thinking that the battle will be easy just because you have asked for the help of Heaven. If anything, you will be tested on every side. Remember, you have an enemy that doesn't want you to succeed. Why? He knows that as you succeed your resources will be given to the advancement of the cause of Christ. This should further fuel your fire to grow your area of assignment as much as you can. The plans and purposes of the Lord are resting on your success!

> **1 Samuel 14:47, "So Saul established is sovereignty over Israel, and fought against all his enemies on every side…"**

The enemy may be present in many different forms. It may be greed, struggles with the economy or within the company, unfair business practices or alliances or an inability to outsmart the competition. Whatever the battle, the king intercepts the enemy on behalf of his kingdom. (or business) It is your job to take the lead and with integrity sound the battle cry for victory.

In order for the king to intercept the enemy forces that will doubtless come his way he must continually seek the counsel of the Lord before he goes to battle. **1 Samuel 23:2 – "Therefore David inquired of the Lord, saying, "Shall I go and attack these Philistines?" And the Lord said to David, "Go and attack the Philistines, and save Keilah.""**

How many times have you found yourself going out to face the competition without even a whisper of a prayer? Do you start a presentation to the stockholders within your own strength? Do you seek the guidance of the Lord to know which contracts will be the most profitable for the company? As you are preparing to respond to a Request for Proposal do you ask His guidance as to which ones are within your grasp? As you are keenly aware by now, business is war. How could you even think of going to battle without the proper preparation? Not only should you be prepared, so should your staff. ***The Principle of Proper Placement*** also means that you allow your battle commanders (management staff) the authority to sound the battle cry or demand more time for proper planning. Have you allowed your staff the autonomy to make decisions regarding the company? If so, don't you think it wise to make sure that you have the right people in places of authority?

It is also important to properly value those employees who operate the day-to-day transactions within the company. While they may not be in the forefront of the battle they are still a vital part of an overall victory plan. These faithful soldiers rarely get the praise and admiration they deserve. Yet, were it not for them, the operation might come to a complete halt. A wise king understands the need for someone to "watch the supplies". (1 Samuel 30:24) This is one of my favorite passages of scripture. It defines what a great leader and manager David was. I encourage you to read the entire 30th chapter as a study on your own. But, for now let me give you a quick run down of the story.

David returns from battling the Philistines with his men to Ziklag only to find that all of their women, children and belongings have been captured by the Amalekites. The account tells us that each of them cried until they had no more strength. Let's stop right there. Some of you may be facing equally devastating news within your own life right now. Can you relate to David and his men? Have you cried out for relief until there are no more words left? Take a deep breath and close your eyes for just a moment. Now, relax in the knowledge that God knows exactly where you are at this very instant. He is with you. Hang on.

We read in verse six that David was getting a bit nervous. He heard that his men were ready to stone him. Ok, I know anyone who has ever been in a business that is going through hard times has felt this way before. You can just imagine your employees pushing you in front of the forklift or tripping you right off the loading dock. Well, that's what David (the great King) was experiencing himself. There was mutiny in the ranks. But, the end of that same verse tells us that he encouraged and strengthened himself in the Lord. Stop trying to do everything on your own. Let faith rise up within you.

What did David do? He prayed and asked God what he should do. The answer was clear. He got the message to go and get back what was stolen from him. So, he and his men started out on the journey to retrieve their belongings. But, along the way some of the men were too exhausted to continue. Remember they had just returned from fighting another battle only to have to get up and ready for the next one. Two hundred of the men stayed behind to watch the supplies. If any of your employees are too tired to face the upcoming battle then let them stay and guard the business and allow those who have the strength to continue. Sometimes, some of your greatest warriors will need a rest.

To make a long story short, David and his men defeated the enemy and retrieved everything that belonged to them along with additional profits. But, as is the case any time you get people involved, some of the men were jealous that David wanted to split everything with all of the men including those who were too weary to continue in the battle. As a good manager you cannot allow this mentality to invade your staff's thinking. They must understand, as David did, that a win for any of them is a win for the whole company. All employees should be able to benefit anytime a victory is won. Every position is just as important as the other.

A wise king realizes that even the "least" of the employees is crucial to the success of the company. Not everyone will be called upon to go to battle or will have the strength for every battle. The king (business owner), manager, department head, must be willing to give his trusted employees a break and still allow them to benefit from the bonus of a business victory. The message must be clear to everyone within the company that teamwork and success are important values within your company structure.

<u>ELEVENTH LESSON</u>: I MUST PLACE PEOPLE WITHIN THEIR AREAS OF EXPERTISE IN ORDER TO GAIN THE MOST BENEFIT FOR THEM AND FOR THE COMPANY.

<u>Questions to consider:</u>

1.) Have you earnestly prayed about the proper placement for all of your employees and for yourself?
2.) Do you know the "sweet spot" where everyone on your team will shine?
3.) Have you consulted God on the strategies needed to make your marketplace thrive?
4.) Do you know your kingdom? (your company and your competition)
5.) Are you willing to intercept the enemy before he gets to you?
6.) Can you name the armor bearer(s) assigned to you?
7.) Have you given God complete control of your kingdom?

Chapter Twelve- The Principle of Vision

What is the Significance of Vision

As we look into the life of your particular placement in the Kingdom, one of the most critical aspects will be the ability to receive and understand the vision that God has for you. If I were to ask you right now what the vision for your future is, would you be able to easily articulate it? What is vision anyway? An easy way to remember the definition is that it is the dream, revelation, idea or mental picture that God has given you regarding your future. If you don't think you know what the vision for your life is at this very moment, don't panic or start hyperventilating yet. Take some deep breaths and calm down. Perhaps God hasn't revealed it to you so far. In fact, most of us can only handle a little bit of the "vision" at a time anyway. If God showed us everything all at once we might not be able to understand it, appreciate it, or be ready to engage in the preparations necessary for it's fulfillment. That is why so many times it takes a lifetime before we truly discover and fulfill our complete destiny.

It's easy in our instant society to want everything all at once. After all, we do live in the fast lane most of the time don't we? Why should God be any different? Why can't He just give us some super sonic dream, lay it all out, and then write on the wall very plainly what He wants us to do. After all, He is God? Ok, I can't be the only one who has ever secretly wished this would happen. But, alas, the time clock of God often beats at an entirely different rhythm. Have you ever wondered why? Well, I have. But, to get the answer we really don't have to go very far. So, before you start begging God for that Mega dream sequence let's take a quick look at what happened to a young man when he stepped out a bit too soon shall we?

You probably have already thought ahead and know who I'm talking about but humor me anyway. It's Joseph. When we catch up with him right after his big dream revelation his life begins to take a very different turn. So after gaining a full respect for this story you might be happy just to get your vision in stages. But, that's for you to decide. ☺

Anyway, Joseph is seventeen, and has a very awesome dream that details some very specific things regarding his future. Suffice it to say in the dream he was the boss and his brothers were bowing down to him and serving him. What's the problem with that you ask? Well, how about that he took the contents of the dream and told the whole enchilada story to his older brothers. Now, unless you live in a fairy land or have a perfect set of siblings this did make for some very tense family moments to put it mildly. Straight talk.....they hated him.....really bad.

Isn't it funny that the brothers always get the bum wrap at this stage of the game? But, come on, let's get real. If one of the younger members of your team who had the least experience of all, came up to you right now and announced to everyone that they were destined to be the boss don't tell me that there might be a little bit of mutiny in the ranks. But, were the contents of Joseph's dream any less true? Absolutely not! Here's the deal, sometimes when you get the vision you need to keep your mouth shut for a while. You need to wait for the time of fulfillment to come. Who's to say? Perhaps if Joseph hadn't blabbed his mouth he could have had a much easier road. To read his entire journey you can look at Genesis chapter 37 and 38. Let's just say his premature revelation cost him some very hard lessons.

What is it about vision that makes everyone so nervous? Well, for starters it usually means that we must transform much of our current nature into something that is far greater than anyone else can imagine. In fact, truth be told, in our own moments of silence we often question the picture that God has placed within us thinking that He surely has meant this for someone else. If you look back over the many journeys that have brought you to where you are right now, would you have seriously wanted to know about some of them in advance? Really?

For some of my little fiascos, I assure you I would have started running and probably never stopped if I would have known everything that it would take to refine me up to this point. I think that is why God in His mercy chooses to give us little chunks at a time. Transformation is painful no matter how you slice it. For most of us the vision God has for us will require a much cleaner, wiser, and purer vessel than we currently portray. That is why it takes His gentle shaping to mold us into the vessel that is fit for our final vision.

So, stop panicking if you don't know everything right now. Much of what Joseph endured didn't make sense at the time he was walking through the valley. But, when he emerged on the other side of the storm he realized that he was placed into that particular moment in history for a specific purpose. To save a remnant of people from annihilation that would become a nation. The same story unfolded for Esther. Her plight led her to a specific moment in history to save her generation from extinction. You may be thinking that your life's mission isn't quite that dramatic or exciting. Is that so? As I see it, you are probably facing a similar scenario in your life right now. You have walked through some very dark places wondering if God truly knew where you were and if He even cared. But, during the process you have grown in character and in wisdom. Why? Perhaps your marketplace is headed for annihilation right now. Maybe you look around and wonder if God's hand of blessing can once again produce a harvest in your devastated harvest field. Well, if that is the case, then it could be that you have been placed in this specific spot in time for a reason. Does your marketplace need a miracle? Then ask for His vision to unfold for you right now.

At some point we have to all bite the bullet so to speak and get a direction for our lives. We have to slow down long enough for God to implant the dream for our future within the very core of our being. It is critical that His vision (revelation for our future) becomes a part of us. There will undoubtedly be obstacles along the way. But, as we pursue our future He will persist in developing His character within us.

If you have ever been in any leadership position you have no doubt experienced the need for vision. People come to you with one question on their mind. "What do you want us to do now?" Have you ever heard these words? What are they really asking? They need direction. That is **why the Word says, "Without a Vision the people perish".**

Someone has to have the courage to take the bull by the horns and start out in a direction. I could give you countless examples of "leaders" who reminded God how much they weren't ready and couldn't do the job. (Moses, Noah, David, Peter, me, you, etc.) But, in his infinite wisdom He ignored who they were at that very moment in time and saw into their destiny. He knew the vision that was before them. He saw their future! That is why He is able to call things that are not as though they were. He sees the person you are to become. Thankfully, He is a God of Vision!

TWELTH LESSON: I MUST SEEK GOD FOR HIS VISION FOR MY MARKETPLACE ACTIVITIES SO THAT HIS WILL CAN BE ACCOMPLISHED THROUGH ME.

Questions to consider:

1.) Do you have a vision for your life right now?
2.) Are there currently things that are keeping you from fulfilling your vision?

3.) Do you ask God to give you His vision for your life and marketplace?
4.) Take a moment right now to write down who you are to become in order to fulfill your destiny.
5.) Start activities that will encourage your vision and strengthen your skill set.
6.) Surround yourself with others who have a like vision and see what the power of that group can do in your life.

Chapter Thirteen- The Principle of Positive Reinforcement

Positive Reinforcement is Critical To Success

To those of you who consider yourself savvy to motivating your team members, you may find yourself thinking you can skip this chapter. However, although this principle may be intuitively obvious to some, it is downright foreign to others. How do I know that? Well, I have worked for people who found it almost impossible to let an encouraging word ever cross their lips. I'm sure you have been there as well. Sadly, you may have been made a public example at some employee meeting or found yourself the brunt of the whisperings within a group of your co-workers. The dialogue from this insensitive person may have reminded you and your department what a miserable failure you have been to the company. Perhaps, you were singled out as the sole source of decreasing profit. Worse yet, maybe you were the individual that was leading the charge to belittle someone into submission. Maybe you are the source of the negativity. Let me ask you a question. Does this make you want to work harder? Well, unless you are a saint, it usually has the same effect on us all. It takes the wind out of our sails. It makes us feel like there is no need to even try further. If you're like me there are momentary thoughts of revenge that develop in your mind. (Ok, I never said I was perfect) Why is

The Principle of Positive Reinforcement so important? Well, to answer that we don't need to look very far. Let's take a peak at how Jesus motivated His team of twelve guys into a secure unit that impacted the world for eternity.

Now let's think about his team for a moment. It was comprised of more than a few characters that you and I probably wouldn't have chosen in the first place. After all, who would want a hot headed fisherman, a tax collector and a person capable of the utmost treachery and betrayal to be part of our management staff? After all, you have to close your eyes sometime! ☺ Yet, despite their human frailties He took them as they were, knowing their faults and formed them into a group that eventually maintained His kingdom after His death and produced a harvest (profit) for all eternity. Not bad for a carpenter and a group of what seemed like ragtag misfits wouldn't you agree? Of course, you may be thinking, yeah but after all He did have divine intervention. But, my friend, so do you! Now, let's get down to motivating our team with ***The Principle of Positive Reinforcement.***

Stop right now, and think for a moment. You may not be in a position of management yet but believe me you are still in a capacity to motivate others no matter what position it is that you occupy. Remember that the next time you try to bounce your teenager out of bed for school after a long night of studying. So, the sooner you learn the power of motivation and the strength that it brings, the easier your life will become. Jesus understood that He had the power to place within His team the confidence necessary to face the future with gusto and an unwavering faith in the final victory. Is your team (family) as confident? Let's look at a few examples.

The first that comes to most of our minds when we think of the flaws in the ranks of the disciples is Peter. He normally gets a bum rap. Most sermons focus on his lack of faith as he begins to sink trying to follow Jesus example of walking on water. However, did you ever think about how much courage it took to step out of the boat in the first place? The fact that he managed to actually walk for a time on the waves is an incredible testament to the inner character of this man. Truth be told many of us would have likely been content to stay in the comfort and safety of the boat.

As we think about the life of Peter, let's also remember that Jesus knew full well what the future held for Him and Peter. He already knew that Peter would deny him at His most critical moment. However, in Matthew 16:17-19 Jesus says,

> **"...Blessed are you, Simon son of Jonah, for this was not revealed to you by man, but by my Father in heaven.**
> **And I tell you that you are Peter, and on this rock I will build my church, and the gates of Hades will not overcome it. I will give you the keys of the kingdom of heaven; whatever you bind on earth will be bound in heaven, and whatever you loose on earth will be loosed in heaven."(Amplified)**

How could Jesus truly look at Peter and declare such a statement over him? Was it faith? Was it wishful thinking? In truth, it was ***The Principle of Positive Reinforcement.*** Jesus knew that there would come a time when Peter would question whether or not there was a divine plan for him. He knew that at Peter's darkest hour of personal defeat he would face the stark reality of failure. He understood that Peter would blame himself as the reason that the crowds were ignited against Jesus. He was a contributing catalyst to the betrayal.

But, Jesus also knew something else. He knew what Peter didn't. He knew that this failure would be a defining moment for his future. He knew that this event would humble Peter and help shape him into a leader that truly would be a rock for the foundation of the gospel message. Jesus knew that Peter could easily succumb in a river of self-defeat. The only thing that could rescue Peter from this pit would be the positive words of affirmation that were spoken over him. He knew that the only thing that could quiet the voices of defeat within Peter's mind would be the positive words of declaration upon which he could reflect. Have you been speaking words of defeat or affirmation over your employees or family? If they were in a moment of despair what words would ring in their mind? Would they be words that could propel them into the greatness of their destiny? If you practice ***The Principle of Positive Reinforcement*** you can inspire those within your sphere of influence to strive for bigger achievements.

This doesn't mean that you never correct negative behavior. All of us need correction at one time or another. In fact, 2 Peter 4:2 declares,

> **"Preach the Word; be prepared in season and out of season; correct, rebuke and encourage with great patience and careful instruction." (Amplified)**

It is a great responsibility to be in a leadership position. You have the power to mold the destiny of those within your kingdom realm. Wow! What an opportunity. What is your primary technique to measure the pulse of the attitude of your company? As you probably see by now I use the pen to help motivate those around me. (and yes, I take a lot of ribbing for it) I have listed below an excerpt for a contribution I sent to our company newsletter. Perhaps it will give you some ideas for the future.

"It's hard to believe that another month has come and gone. But, alas, time does have a way of sneaking up on us doesn't it? It is easy to get caught up in the hurried pace of our everyday lives. If you're like me there are moments when you arrive at your destination and you can't remember how you even got there. (ok, I know I'm not the only one that has these senior moments) Here's another little secret that I try to keep to myself. I have actually dialed the phone and then forgot who it was I was trying to talk to in the first place. What's even worse is that when you finally figure out who's on the other end you can't remember why you called them. Why does this happen? Well, other than the fact that I am older than dirt as some of my team reminds me, I think part of it largely reflects the multitasking that I find is necessary in any given day. I'm sure many of you can relate.

One of the great things about working in a small company is the sense of family that each of us has for the other. There is a special bond that allows all of our many varied personalities to come together and form what we lovingly refer to as the team. However rewarding those moments are, we also get to experience first hand some of the challenges that are a direct reflection of our "family" environment. Remember the little dialogue we just had about multi tasking? Well, guess what? Name any other person in the company and I can promise you that they too are wearing multiple hats. They are experiencing the same frustration and all out panic at times that you feel as they try to satisfy the demands of our customers. What's the significance of this revelation? Well, just before you get ready to pounce on someone because you may be having a hard day, take a moment to consider that their day has probably had an equal amount of struggle as well. As in any family there will be times when one person may have to pull a bit more of the load, but, as time marches forward we will each have our moment and opportunity of martyrdom. You know what I mean don't you? I'm talking about those long dialogues that people give you about how the building would burn down and the company would fold if they weren't part of the team. Just look at that person and smile and give them their moment in the limelight of martyrdom syndrome. If it lasts too long, then slap them lightly and tell them to get over themselves. We each have our own impact and purpose within the company. That's what makes us a team. We need each other.

Why is all of this so important you ask? Well, like it or not, we are a team, and as such, need to operate as one. It's give and take. It's life. Let's all be willing to roll up our sleeves, get our hands dirty, and help each other to provide the best possible product and service to our customers. Are some customers ridiculously demanding? YES. Do some of the requests they make seem unfair or downright illogical? YES. But, at the end of the day, they are the bosses that contribute to all of our paychecks. That should help each of you see the high maintenance customers in a different light. Every time you catch yourself dreaming of ways to eliminate that customer, pull your paycheck out, look it over real good, and remember who helped add those little zeros behind the number. That should help us all. Believe me, there are days when there aren't enough aspirin in the world to reduce the pounding in my head from a hard day. But, again, we are a team working together to provide the customer with the best quality and service that they have ever received.

We are proud of each of you. We are honored that you have made our family part of yours. We look forward to the many great things that are in our future. We are in the process of gaining new certifications and product specialties that will allow us to grow as a company and as individuals. Since our stated mission is to be the provider of choice for any IT infrastructure decision and the standard by which others are measured, we have a lot to work toward. I would humbly like to ask each of you a final question. At the end of the day as you are packing up to leave, take one last look around your workspace. Will the product and service that you are leaving the customer for that days work be a testament to your abilities and to our company's mission statement? If not, for the sake of our family, can you take a moment to tidy up your area, make that one last phone call or send that extra email? Why? Well, if all of us together, added that one extra little effort at the end of the day the impact that our customers would experience would be astronomical. Sometimes, it's the little things that separate us from all of our competitors. Next time you watch the Indy 500 look what a difference one tenth of a second can make. We each have the ability to give one tenth of a second more don't we? It may be the difference between winning and losing.

Once again, thanks for the contributions that each of you make. We need every single one of you to make our family complete. Keep up the good work! We've had a great history in the past, we are growing in the present, and the future looks brighter than ever. Now, together let's put that one tenth of a second to the test this month shall we? Watch and see what a difference it will make!"

Now, I know what some of you may be thinking. How sappy can one person get? The answer is very. These are real life examples of what I use in my position at work. These are not theories that are in some textbook waiting for some trail period. These are tested in the fire of my own workplace journey. So, you see my friend, I too am in the trenches with you. I understand what you are going through right now. I know what it means to be shouldering the burden of management while still needing to promote the welfare of those within your department. As a boss, I hope I put the needs of my department ahead of my own. No matter how many deadlines I may be facing, and gross profit reports that I have due, I must be willing to sacrifice my needs for the sake of those on my team.

If you aren't the leader yet, don't worry, your time will come I assure you. So, no matter what your particular position may be at this moment in time, you must learn ***The Principle of Positive Reinforcement*** if you are going to build a team for the future. Your marketplace depends on the loyalty, support and respect of those around you. They must know that you believe in them even if they make mistakes. They need to feel the comfort of knowing they can express their opinion even if it differs from your own without getting their head removed. You must make every effort (and sometimes it will be an effort) to remind them how special they are to you. When was the last time you reminded those around you how important they are with a simple hand written note of thanks? Well, neighbor, that may be too long! Give it a try. Jesus took every opportunity to point out the positive things within those He was privileged to lead. Even after Peter's dismal failure He spoke a word of encouragement to declare that Peter would have a profound influence on the future church. That took eyes of faith. But, with ***The Principle of Positive Reinforcement*** all things are possible.

THIRTEENTH LESSON: I MUST LEARN TO SPEAK WORDS THAT WILL INSPIRE MY TEAM TO THE GREATNESS THAT IS INSIDE EACH OF THEM.

Questions to consider:

1.) Do you spend your time building your team up or tearing them down?
2.) Do you have regular meetings to praise your team publicly and privately?

3.) When was the last time you sent a hand written note of thanks to those that are within your marketplace?
4.) Can you truly say that you operate within this principle right now?
5.) If not, what steps can you take to start praising your team?

Chapter Fourteen- The Principle of Paying Attention

Paying Attention is one of the most profitable lessons you will learn.

Ok, all of us at some point in our life have wanted to grab someone by the arm, pull them close and ask them in the loudest voice that decorum will allow…."will you look at me and pay attention!" Don't try to say that the inner desire to achieve this doesn't happen to you at least once a week. What is it about human nature that it seems that something has to hit us smack dab over our heads before we stop long enough to pay attention? Oh, I know your excuse. You're busy doing things for the Lord, right? Well, my friend, try that excuse on someone else. ☺ The only reason I can joke with you now is because I have used that excuse many times myself, and it just doesn't seem to fly anymore. Some of you are so busy doing "things" that you haven't heard the still small voice of a loving Heavenly Father in a very long time. In fact, some of you haven't even heard the siren that is going off deep in your inner man right now. How do I know? I've been there. Recently.

The other morning in one of my devotionals I think I had a siren experience. Proverbs 24:33 says, **"I applied my heart to what**

I observed and learned a lesson from what I saw." For whatever reason I had that audible "duh" experience creep up on me where I realized that God had been trying to say something for a long time and I was just too thick headed to get it. God had been trying to show me through practical examples how easy it is to get sidetracked and/or complacent in the battle for our marketplace. For most of us we fall into a comfortable routine and relax our defenses and coast a bit. (Caution: In sales coasting is not allowed unless you want to starve!) In comparison, in a true battle situation relaxing our defense is not an option either unless we want to face our death a bit sooner than planned. Yet, slowing and subtley the enemy is encroaching upon our territory each and every day. He takes inches one day and feet the next. Many times he does this right under our noses. At these vulnerable times it happens at such a slow pace that we barely notice it until it's almost too late.

This particular morning the Lord got through to me and began to show me "lessons" that I had missed along the way. How much easier it would have been if I would have just paid attention the first time around. His message was loud and clear. **IT IS MUCH EASIER TO CONQUER TERRITORY IN FORWARD MOTION THAN IT IS TO DEFEND IT WHILE IN RETREAT!** Wow, what a lesson that was. Why? When we are advancing on the enemy he is on the defense, not us. Do you get it? Look around you right now and pay attention to what you see. Ask yourself a question. Are you ready? Here is the million-dollar question. "Am I on the offense or defense?" Simple question. God speaks to you every day. Do you listen? Remember the Proverb from a moment ago? Let's look at it again. **"I applied my heart to what I observed and learned a lesson from what I saw." (Proverbs 24:33)**

<u>There are two ways to learn in your marketplace.</u>

1.) You can learn from your mistakes.
2.) You can learn from those around you.

If you are like me (and I'm sure you are) you are going to make mistakes along the way. Get over it. Learn from it. In fact, be the first one to admit that you messed up. People who can accept responsibility for their actions have the confidence necessary to begin the offensive attack. If you are secure in who you are then you can allow God to take your mistakes and show you how to sharpen your skills. Close your eyes (after you read this section) and visualize a target at the end of a narrow field. Look at the target and study it for just a moment. Can you see that there are many "areas" within that one target that will allow you to score? Stop right here for just a moment. Some of you are so dead set that a bulls eye is the only way to really rack up any points that you miss the journey totally. You are paralyzed in fear and thus choose to do nothing. One thing is certain. If you aren't willing to settle for "a score" then no war can ever be won. Wars are made up of several battles along the way. The point is…..stay in the game. Sometimes, just managing to score will make the difference in winning or losing.

Sorry, I digressed onto my small soapbox for a moment. Let's go back to our target practice shall we? Now, picture yourself standing just far enough away to still be able to clearly see the target ahead. In your hand is the most exquisite bow and arrow that money can buy. The targeting mechanism has been hand crafted and expertly designed for your particular stature and aim. You are guaranteed a hit with this set up. Now, pick up the bow, place the arrow, and take aim at your target. Gently pull back on the bow, aim and fire! Watch as the arrow sails to the target ahead. See the arrow striking with a surety that defines that moment in time. Stay in that moment as you look at the target. Did you hit it? Of course you did. Why? The difference was made when you stopped long enough to prepare and see the battle ahead. Is it any different in life?

Yet, strangely we often find ourselves running through life so much on rote that we miss the joy of the journey altogether. That is why the enemy will try to make sure that you become comfortable in your surroundings. It is critical that you understand the reasoning behind this strategy. The more battles you win the greater your reflection ability. What does that mean? In times of our deepest trials we can find peace in remembering other victories of battles long past or newly won. The longer we allow time to pass between each battle advancement, the greater the danger for us to fall into the trap of stagnation. Anything stagnant stinks. Are you at a place in your marketplace where you haven't felt the power of progression in a while? It is what I refer to as the "whatever" state of mind. When you find yourself thinking that "whatever" happens it really doesn't matter you better run back to your prayer closet post haste and ask for some renewed passion and zeal. Whatever won't get you anywhere that is worth going. Remember, specific directions produce specific outcome. How long has it been since you have applied your heart to what you have been shown? Perhaps the current situation you find yourself in has already been answered for you (if you would have just been paying attention).

Believe me I understand the weariness that forward development brings. It can be exhausting. That is why it is vital to your success to follow the steps that we have already talked about in the previous chapters. Let your team take the lead once in a while. If you have been the kind of leader that makes progress possible, then a little rest now and then is allowed. They can carry the ball for you. It doesn't always have to be you that carries the ball for the touchdown. Stop trying to be the glory hound. You just have to stay on the team and stay engaged. What is the last lesson you remember the Lord speaking to you? Has it been recently? Are you listening? Sometimes our greatest achievements are paying attention to the things that surround us. Once you see the lesson then apply it. What does that mean? In simple terms it means to allow it to become a part of what defines you. If we would pay attention more and apply what we learn, the voyage through work and life would seem much less rocky.

FOURTEENTH LESSON: IT IS MUCH EASIER TO CONQUER TERRITORY IN FORWARD MOTION THAN IT IS TO DEFEND IT WHILE IN RETREAT.

Questions to consider:

1.) Do you keep a journal of life lessons that God is teaching you?

2.) Do you apply your heart to new revelations and work to incorporate them into your life?
3.) Do you keep in a forward motion for advancement in your marketplace?
4.) Do you pay attention to your surroundings and ask God for divine wisdom to interpret the signs?

Chapter Fifteen - The Principle of A United Front

Positive Reinforcement is the key to any successful team.

Have you ever really wondered what was meant by the term "United Front"? Actually, this term has been around for centuries and has been used as a strategy of war throughout time. So, if you want to build a truly WINNING company let's break it down a bit for purposes of understanding, shall we? According to Webster's dictionary to unite means to bring into close connection. (Webster's dictionary, page 351) In the same reference book the word front means the appearance or demeanor or the area of activity. (Webster, pg. 184) I encourage you to take a journey through history for more specific examples. Perhaps a study of the great battle tactics of Alexander the Great would help you. But, for now let's just keep it simple shall we?

Historically speaking, the term "United Front" has probably been around since the dawn of time. We can read of similar tactics used by the Israelites, the Great Persian Army, and even America's war for independence just to name a few. The technique of the united front was defined as a military tactical alliance between two parties who normally found it difficult to agree on anything. (Sound familiar yet?) Do you have departments within your own company that can't even agree on something as simple as the dress code or how to answer the phone? If so, how do you plan on conquering your marketplace?

This particular approach is to allow each unit to remain independent, while at the same time working together around common issues, in hopes that such a union would promote a larger platform for change. Why should battle strategies of centuries gone by still bring out your respect and consideration? The simple truth is that you are in a war every day to win against your competitor in a very hostile market. If you have not witnessed or felt the winds of war blowing on your half of the parade, hang tight, they will.

If I were to take each of you aside at this very moment I would dare say that a large percentage of you could easily spout off many things about your company, management, or your fellow workers that you would love to transform. After all, transformation is a wonderful process, isn't it? (especially when it's happening to someone else) Perhaps a "little makeover" is all they need. But, before we all get so quick to begin this procedure, let's stop for just a moment and really think. What really started me on this quest regarding a "United Front" in the first place? (Besides the fact that I can't sleep) I recently began thinking about some comments within my own work environment that disturbed me deeply. Now stop right now before you hasten to think that I, in some form or fashion, believe myself to be some sort of saint. I will spare you that thought. I don't. I do however believe that I have a responsibility as a leader within the company I serve to make commentaries and adjustments where need be, if we are truly to become a company that we can all be proud to call home. **To ignore is easy. To illicit change is difficult.**

Next time you want to throw stones at your supervisor or the owner of the company just remember that they are probably the ones that can't sleep at night if they don't have the benefit of the principles that we have discussed thus far to comfort and guide them. I'm sure at times they feel as if the sails on their ships are totally out of steam. Let me share with you briefly something I just shared with the staff of the company where I currently serve as Vice-President of Sales. Consider it my "Rah Rah" speech to motivate the troops on the very subject of this chapter. See, there are practical uses for these principles!

As a letter to all employees I included the following observations. Perhaps they may help you as you seek to guide your staff toward a common goal. I reminded our team, "If you still haven't noticed the changes taking place, believe me our competitors have. Let's point back to our mission statement. We all see it everyday on every wall in the building! We say it at every company gathering so I'll spare you the speech for now. Suffice it to say that we are all about customer satisfaction and quality. I received a call over the weekend that just had to make me smile. A rep from another company called me to tell me that we had gotten our greatest opponent really running and on the defense. This person was commenting that they couldn't seem to beat us anywhere and it really irked them that we were getting a reputation of being the first again. The first at what you ask? We were the first to employ an outside auditing firm to come in and do the quality checks on our jobs. We allow our customers free access to them to ensure a comfort factor that is second to none in our industry. It allows us absolute autonomy and virtually ensures that the "good ole' boy" system doesn't play favorites where our quality of work is concerned. That same adversary is now inquiring as to how much it will cost to put such a measure in place at their company. (Only six months too late, I must add) We are the first to embrace new Homeland Security Technology in an ever changing world.

I get calls from competitors (Yes, competitors), manufacturers, trainers and the like, all commenting on changes we have made, our positive progression, and on each of you. So, lest you think I am full of some great wisdom I would like to quote the words of the greatest leader known to man. Just remember that His team of seemingly misfits and hot heads are still changing the lives of many today despite the fact that their management techniques were taught over 2000 years ago. I'm not egotistical enough to believe that I can improve on those odds. However, He said in Matthew 12:25 "...Every kingdom divided against itself is brought to desolation, and every city or house divided against itself **WILL NOT** stand." (Jesus Christ) It still speaks volumes today. If you, as a member of this company, raise your voice in mock disdain or in a commentary that is less than flattering about your fellow worker then you can bet a nail somewhere in our foundation has just gotten loosened a bit. Every time you choose to call someone else by a name or laugh at the joke at lunch about how stupid and incompetent another department is, then just visualize the beam supporting our structure cracking just a little more.

Why do I care? I want to remind you that each one of you is just as important as the company that employs us all. First, as a leader I must apologize for any time that I may have found myself agreeing with or at least not putting a halt to such behavior. Sometimes, in moments of frustration we all say and do stupid things. But, I want all of you to look within yourself at this moment and ask one question. Am I perfect? If you are then please run (Don't walk) to HR and get your name on the next promotion list. If not, then join the rest of us. Again, why am I babbling on about a "United Front"? Because I have seen, and so have some of our vendors as of late, that we have lost our edge. What edge you ask? The one we used to have. The one where we truly believe that all of us were put in this company for a specific reason and how much we each need the other to complete our mission in the workplace.

Somehow over the past few years there seems to be a shift of thinking. Operations thinks sales and estimating can't get their way out of a paper bag. Sales and estimating think that operations can't find the bag to begin with. (Or this is what I'm hearing) Do you realize that every time you allow yourself the luxury of speaking against your fellow worker you are destroying the very company we are all building? You weaken our foundation. You crack the slab. You chip away at another nail. Well, you get the picture. When it's among "our" family it's bad enough and we should be ashamed. But, when we take it beyond these doors to the cruel world of competition, it is nothing short of shameful. Why? Because our enemy has learned long ago that a house divided against itself will not stand. They pay attention to any inner fighting, sly innuendos, or quick accusations. If they find these, then they know there is a crack somewhere. They are not worried about the superstars we have. (And yes we have some) They are worried about us joining together for the common good

("United Front") and kicking them all the way back from where they came . This, my dear friends, is their deepest fear. Are you up to the hardest task of all? Well, here it is. STOP TALKING! Improper bidding won't kill us. Operational mistakes won't take us under. But, if we don't even like each other as a team.......now that will sink us quicker than boots filled with quick sand.

As one of your leaders, I would like to remind you once again that each of you has a place that only you can fill. You were put here for a reason. As frustrated as we all may get with one another, it is critical that we keep those same frustrations inside our own home and allow them to strengthen us. Can you master your own emotions? Can you turn the tide of defeatism that is lapping at our door? I believe you can. I try to live by a simple philosophy. I need the talent and input of those around me. It helps keep me humble. Humility is a lesson each of us should practice.

Why is this all so important? The survival of the company may depend on each of our abilities to keep our opinions to ourselves. Remember, each of you is here to do a job and hopefully, have fun in the process. Let's remind each other what a great team we have during this Thanksgiving Season. I'm proud to be part of this company. I'm proud to call each of you family. Thanks for everything you do to help us move forward and to all the great things that await us in the many victories ahead."

This was taken from a letter that I sent out to the entire staff the week of Thanksgiving. Even great companies need to be reminded now and again that the old adage that loose lips sink ships still holds true today. If you are a leader within your company, department, church, or family it is critical that you clearly understand the importance of a united front. It confuses your enemy. (Competition) They know the strength that occurs when agreement takes place. Remember, it was the Lord who reminded us that any two people agreeing on one thing brings a commitment of victory. Why? Think about it. How hard do you find it to keep two people agreeing together on one thing for the long haul? Do you see the power? Imagine if the entire group, department or company could rally under the same banner and push forward together. It would truly be an unstoppable force. Do you need an edge right now? Are you looking for a new device that will take you to the next level? Why not try the simple age-old strategy of a united front. It will surprise you what a group of focused, committed people can do. All we have to do is look at twelve ordinary men who united for one purpose and see what a difference they made in history. Are you ready to make your mark? Are you ready to lead your company to greatness? Master ***The Principle of the United Front***!

FIFTEENTH LESSON: A UNITED FRONT WILL CONFUSE MY ENEMY.

Questions to consider:

1.) Do you consider the unity within your ranks as you go about your daily activities?
2.) Do you allow other team members (family members) to talk trash about their fellow workers?
3.) Do you find yourself speaking bad about others that are on your team instead of discussing it with them personally?
4.) Have you determined that a united front is the key to forward advancement against your enemy? I encourage you to study some of the major battles in history for inspiration.

Chapter Sixteen - The Principle of Perception

The Principle of Perception is vital for success.

I have saved one of my favorite tools for success for our last principle. Once an individual really gets a handle on the power of perception then they truly become an unstoppable force. For you see, most people only consider what they believe to be true in a situation. Sadly, truth is rarely the key ingredient. It doesn't matter what may be happening all around you. But, it does matter a great deal about what the perceived circumstances are. Why? Well, for starters, most of those we deal with on a daily basis are reacting on what they perceive is transpiring as opposed to the actual event. How many times have you been blindsided by a situation because someone "perceived" that something else was taking place other than what actually was?

Perception is everything. It controls the tide of opinion. It controls the emotional balance of the environment. It levels the playing field of competition. Why? Things aren't always as they seem are they? How many times have you reacted to an event based on perception only to find out later that the truth held an entirely different story? As humans we often blaze into a situation without having all of the facts at our disposal. (surely I'm not the only one that does that) At times this passion for swiftness is due to the perception of foul play, or altered outcomes. Why can't we learn to balance logic and truth into our equations before reacting? Well, it's is because perception is a powerful tool. It can make even the most stoic tremble at the vain imaginations that it brings.

What is perception really? It is a combination of observations and the discernment that is associated with its implications. If you were with me on a regular basis you would find that I am often heard reiterating that perception is everything. It causes us to make assumptions that are often totally off base. Have you ever misread an event because of the perception of what was going on? That is why the Bible warns us to shun the very appearance of evil. The reason is clear. Perception is reality to many. Sadly, many friendships, families and partnerships have been broken due to the assumptions made based on perceived unscrupulous activities. Completely innocent events have become a tangled web of misunderstandings that damage and complicate situations needlessly. So, what's the answer?

I instruct those on my staff to first consider how perception may play a role in the handling of an angry customer, a wounded friend, or an irate co-worker. The environment may easily be perceived as hostile when in fact there was no ill will intended. Don't be easily swayed off guard by this little culprit. Start analyzing things in your life from the pure aspect of perception. It will open a new world for you. It will allow you to separate your emotions from most stressful situations. It is one of the easiest ways to find understanding in sometimes complicated circumstances.

Was there ever a time in the life of Jesus that he ignored the perception to walk in faith? When I think of this I am reminded of the little outing that He took with His disciples in the boat during a nasty storm. According to the account everyone in the boat (except Jesus) was fairly certain that they were going to drown the storm was so bad. They were basing their decision solely on what they observed. But, thankfully, God doesn't look at situations based on perception. He looks at the deeper level of truth with an eye of faith. We tend to spend our time analyzing the things we can see. God looks at all the things that can't be seen with the natural eye. Clearly, He sees what we don't. We speak about what is. **He speaks to what will be**. That is why Jesus was able to stand in confidence during that storm and speak peace to the storm. The disciples addressed the storm. They took their observations and made their commentaries accordingly. Jesus ignored what was in the present to speak to what He wanted in the future. He spoke to Peace and said, **Be Still**. Wow! Maybe it's time you stop speaking to what is and speak to what you want to have in your future. Get it? Stop reacting to everything that is going on around you and start building on faith.

Do you find yourself in a place in your business where you feel totally hopeless and outnumbered? Well, if that is where you are right now, let me encourage you with a vital lesson on how important the power of perception is to the ultimate outcome of your particular battle. Let's look at a great warrior in the Bible shall wc? Let me set the stage for you. The story is found in Judges Chapter seven. Gideon is trying to form his army to face the Midianites. He starts with thousands and through a process of elimination ends up with 300 men. (Read the story. It is fascinating. Sounds like a movie doesn't it?) It is not the normal battle strategy of a military man. Usually, a military man wants to face these odds with an overwhelming force. But, God had a greater purpose in mind. In fact, in verse two, He lets Gideon know that He is going to minimize the number of warriors so that all of Israel will know that the victory was by the hand of the Lord. So, look around, if there are only a few of you still standing, take heart, victory is just around the corner.

Well, to make a very long story short, Gideon ends up with a very small contingent of men to face a formidable enemy. Think of the Midianites as your competition at the moment. Imagine yourself surrounded (not hard for some of you). Then, God does the unthinkable. He gives an unusual battle command. He instructs Gideon to divide the men into three groups and go against the enemy with a trumpet, empty pitchers, and torches inside the pitchers. Come on, think with me here. If you were Gideon, what would you be thinking? Has God ever asked you to face your competition with tools you thought were not adequate? Well, I'm sure Gideon was no exception. Imagine the guys on the front lines! But, when the battle began, they blew the trumpets, broke the pitchers and started shouting a battle cry. It so confused the enemy that they turned on each other. Why? The Principle of Perception was at work. It appeared that a great army was coming against them. Wow! If God has the power to take a few hundred men and defeat a vast army, don't you think He can handle your situation right now?

Do you ever find yourself cutting corners or treating alliances with a flippancy that could easily be misconstrued? Do you ever partake in activities that seem harmless enough but on deeper inspection could simply send the wrong message? Why does this matter? As you are tidying up your marketplace to ensure that everything is built on a solid foundation it is very important that you also consider the subtle messages you are sending on a regular basis. This is the perception by which you will be judged. Is it fair? Probably not. But, it is that perceived message that will be read loud and clear by those who are evaluating your marketplace. If you will learn the simple rule of watching what perception signals you are sending then there will be a lot less explaining and apologizing that you will have to do in your future. Put out a message that breaths life into those that are so desperately looking for a harvest of blessing. Remember, in the world of commerce perception is everything. What signals have you been sending lately? What conclusions have you jumped to this week needlessly that may have sapped your energy and your joy? Start paying attention to perception. It is one of your most powerful tools.

SIXTEENTH LESSON: PERCEPTION IS EVERYTING.

Questions to consider:

1.) Do you pay attention to the signals you are sending?
2.) Do you consider how something could have been perceived before your react to a situation?

3.) Do you consider the perception that your employees, customers and vendors may have of you as you approach your marketplace?

Marketplace Conclusion

Wow, what a ride we have been on together. I hope it's been challenging yet fun. By now I hope you have a firm grasp on how much God wants to participate in your marketplace. He is keenly interested in everything that concerns you. Stop right now and reflect on some of the things we have shared together.

We have learned how to build a proper foundation and go out with our full body armor. We have discovered how God can transform even our darkest moments into great triumphs for His kingdom advancement. He wants to use His creative force to breathe life into our deflated profit markets and open doors into new territories for us to conquer.

As we dedicate our lives to His control and follow His proven economy we no longer need to be a slave to the trappings of economic trends. We can step into our marketplace authority and walk into the wealth that He has in store for us. As long as we remain accountable for our actions and keep our covenants then God's supernatural favor is sure to engulf our every endeavor. We can find our perfect placement in His kingdom and strive to fulfill the vision that is ordained for us thereby bringing transformation and restoration to everyone within our sphere of influence.

Through positive reinforcement and paying attention to our surroundings we can build a team that presents a united front that can storm the opposition and take them off guard. We can use the art of perception to allow a full representation of our marketplace to unfold and speak words of life into all we put our hand to achieve.

What is it you want right now? Do you have a clearer picture of who you are in Christ and what He wants to bring to pass through you? Will you use the principles we just shared together to refine your workplace journey to make it more acceptable and pleasing to the Father? If you are ready for what God has in store, then He is more than able and ready to jump start you right now. He stands with arms outstretched and is covering you right now. It is His will for you to be blessed as you prepare and present to Him a marketplace that is worthy of His presence. It is my sincere prayer that this book has been a blessing and has ignited a spark and light of hope within your heart. Your future is bright! Now, let's go out there together and transform our cities, our workplaces, our families, and our nations for the Kingdom of God. How will we do it? One day at a time!

May His richest blessings overtake you in the entire journey that is ahead. Thank you for allowing me to spend this time with you. It has been my honor and privilege to share part of the journey with you. Remember the Kingdom rule that God is preparing for you is meant to last forever! Now, aren't you ready to walk into the destiny that God has prepared for you? He's with you all the way!

Daniel 2:44
"In the time of those kings, the God of heaven WILL set up a kingdom that will never be destroyed; nor will it be left to another people. It will crush all those kingdoms and bring them to an end, but it will itself endure forever."

Paula White

P.O.B 25151 Tampa

zip - 33622

$35.00

1800- 992 8892

P.W.org

Printed in the United States
104396LV00003B/284/A

9 780615 16493